The Lohman Way

Entrepreneur Lowell Lohman's
Story and Strategies for Building
Multimillion-Dollar Family Businesses

By
E.L. Wilks

Copyright, 2017
Lowell Lohman and Nancy Lohman

The Lohman Way

Entrepreneur Lowell Lohman's
Story and Strategies for Building
Multimillion-Dollar Family Businesses

All Rights Reserved

No text or images in this book
may be used or reproduced in any
manner without written permission
of the copyright holders.

Cover layout and interior
layout by Capri Porter.

Printed in the United States of America

ISBN: 978-0-9972523-8-5

Published by Legacies & Memories
St. Augustine, Florida

(888) 862-2754
www.LegaciesandMemories.com
www.LegaciesandMemoriesPublishing.com

*Have a tremendous blend of power and warmth.
It's the perfect combination in business.*

– Lowell Lohman

Contents

Introduction

Chapter 1
Teach and Share...11

Chapter 2
Born to Lead...21

Chapter 3
Life Detour...33

Chapter 4
Calculated Risks...39

Chapter 5
'If You Can't Close, You Can't Sell'...49

Chapter 6
'Stop the World'...69

Chapter 7
Sales Managers, 'Try Saying Thank You'...79

Chapter 8
Think of the Possibilities...93

Chapter 9
'You Have to Make Things Happen'...109

Chapter 10
Beginnings...115

Chapter 11
New Life...121

Chapter 12
'Every Business Has a Moment'...163

Chapter 13
'If You're Giving Back, It's Such a Great Feeling'...185

Chapter 14
'Jump on These Shoulders and Hang On'...193

Sources and References...201

Appendices...205
Lowell Lohman's Acknowledgments...207
Important Dates...209
Summary of Achievements...211

Index...213

About The Author...217

Introduction

Lowell Lohman is certain that his business success spanning more than five decades stems from lessons he learned in his childhood and teenage years. Many came from sports, where being a leader seemed to come naturally to him. Growing up in a family with supportive and loving parents also provided encouragement to Lowell and his two younger brothers, and taught them and shaped them into young men of character. His parents emphasized the importance of strong family bonds – still present today as the brothers are as close as ever.

Even as much as Lowell's parents and coaches believed in him and believed in his potential, it's doubtful they ever imagined, just as he never imagined, the kind of success he would achieve in life and business. Fittingly, most of it has revolved around family – owning and operating businesses with family members, including, at various times, Lowell's mother and his stepfather; two brothers; his youngest son; and Lowell's wife. Over the years, together they built businesses worth more than $250 million.

Lowell did well creating and building some of those businesses by himself. Along the way, while working to endure and overcome recessionary obstacles, some stumbles taught him valuable lessons that proved their worth later in his business career. He also had some setbacks and a few rocky relationships in his personal life, but he overcame most of those.

For much of his life, he has found the greatest potential, success and enjoyment in family businesses. He truly loves working with family members. And as the one who has always been the most entrepreneurial and the one most willing to take risks, he has usually been the force behind the creation and growth of various companies. Still, he acknowledges he would never have achieved the kind of success in business or in his personal life without the key roles family members have had, and still have.

Through decades of experience and learning, Lowell's strategies, business philosophy and sales and management practices have worked well regardless of the type of company or industry. And many can be used by other entrepreneurs. But even before he developed those practices, there were other important factors and traits at work. Those, too, can be learned by others. In addition, Lowell's wife, Nancy, who has been one of his business partners since 1996, has strategies and management practices she has applied. Those also are included in this chronicle.

Lowell's story and his family's story will resonate with most people in business – entrepreneurs, as well as individuals with entrepreneurial aspirations, especially if they want to own a business, or multiple businesses, with family.

The Lohman Way

Chapter 1

Teach and Share
Ormond Beach, Florida
April 13, 2017

"Work is an extension of personality. It is achievement. It is one of the ways in which a person defines himself, measures his worth, and his humanity."
Peter F. Drucker

Lowell Lohman is still the quarterback *and* cheerleader – fifty-five years since making plays and throwing high school words of encouragement. Nearly thirty years since leading and cheering grown men to a national championship in flag football. Time has not altered his leadership DNA, although the focus changed from sports to business, and he no longer wears number 11. Now, his uniform is business attire.

The seventy-two-year-old entrepreneur steps to a lectern situated atop a long table in a small room where about thirty employees have just been served lunch. For the next hour, during his informal speech, Lowell will be the analytical business owner, a proud and sometimes critical boss, a motivational speaker and a father figure, dispensing practical ideas for business along with sage advice for life frequently wrapped in aphorisms that have come to be known as "Lowellisms." Quotes and wisdom about business, about life. Some original, some perhaps not so original, although still passages that stand the test of time and impart messages often found in books about business or philosophy or psychology.

"Average is not good enough."

"Today is the day."

"Under-promise. Over-deliver."

Lowell, along with his wife, Nancy, and his youngest son, Ty, are here for a quarterly meeting with their local and regional apartment managers and maintenance supervisors who operate the eleven apartment complexes the Lohmans own in Florida. Nearly twenty-five hundred apartments in Jacksonville, Daytona Beach and Orlando.

Until a few years ago, owning apartment buildings was not something Lowell ever considered. But entrepreneurs don't sit on the sideline of opportunity. And for Lowell, that's especially true when it means being involved in yet another family business. With a few exceptions, Lowell's teams have been various family members in multiple businesses during the past five decades. They are the reason he made his foray into the cemetery business in the 1970s, and then into the funeral business in the 1980s, which led him to become a millionaire – and then later, earn many more millions before making even more money in the apartment business.

Owning apartment buildings, he says, is even better than owning funeral homes and cemeteries, and it's special because he and his wife and son own the company. Ty started the business, and as it began to grow, he asked Lowell and Nancy to invest and be part of the company. Like his father, Ty enjoys being in business with family. His wife, Tovah, a real estate broker, assists Ty in their individual real estate holdings.

At today's meeting, Lowell is in his element – and

with only slight hints of nervousness. Like a performer in the spotlight, he enjoys being on stage. He's accustomed to giving speeches and informal talks to employees, and sometimes to large groups, always happy for the opportunity to talk about systems, monitoring and other business practices he deems crucial for a company to succeed. In the context of public speaking, Lowell and the other Lohmans often tell a story about golfer Jack Nicklaus. After Nicklaus won his last Master's Tournament, he was asked how he handled the pressure knowing millions were watching him attempt to make a ten-foot putt. His response, Lowell says, was, "Are you kidding me? That is what I live for." During the few seconds before Lowell or Nancy or Ty stand to give a speech, they whisper to each other: "It's Jack Nicklaus time." And what each of them is thinking, Lowell says, is, "This is your moment. Kick butt! This is what you live for…. You will do great."

Of course, Lowell loves the opportunity to give speeches about business, but he also sees his role as the company's cheerleader offering words of encouragement and inspiration.

> *LOWELL'S INSIGHT*
>
> **Leadership**
> Leadership is not about you. It's about making other people better. Leadership is more about the trust you have earned than the authority you have been granted.
> The leadership foundation stems from one thing: the ability of an individual to establish a following among other individuals or teams. Know your team and yourself well; have confidence and courage; build the next generation of leaders; actively listen; be organized and structured; share credit with others; and inspire others to do things.

With Ty seated to his right, Nancy to his left, and employees all around the main table and several side tables, the attention is on Lowell. He no longer looks like a quarterback, although he is still trim and fit. He is the mature and graying leader. Today he is dressed elegantly but casually in dark slacks, a light-colored dress shirt, a black-gray patterned sportscoat, and shiny black Versace loafers.

> ## LOWELL'S INSIGHT
>
> **Lead with Vision**
> Leading means having a vision and sharing it with others. Only when you get to inspire others is it possible to share a common goal toward directing the efforts and dedication of the entire team.
> The definition of leadership goes on forever. You must constantly be developing the leaders around you, consistently training, working as a team to reach a common goal, having the enthusiasm to inspire other people.

Giddy with excitement, as if he just tossed a game-winning touchdown, he's anxious to talk about stellar results: Last month, nine of the eleven apartment complexes set records for gross income. As he calls the names of select individuals, he asks each one to stand. Then, the real fun begins, for them – and for Lowell.

Bring out the stack of $100 bills.

It's difficult to tell who is more excited, the employees or Lowell. He truly loves giving out $100 bills – to employees, to servers at restaurants, to the unsuspecting. It's his way of practicing random acts of kindness, or in this case, showing appreciation for a job well-done. For the unexpected who have never seen him carry out this play, it's tangible evidence of rewarding employees for exemplary work. But even for those who have seen Lowell distribute hundreds of dollars like there's no tomorrow, it's still a welcomed and greatly appreciated gesture because, well, a $100 bill is more than just a piece of green paper featuring a stoic Benjamin Franklin. Within minutes, employees have received a total of $1,000 conveying a message worth many times that amount. And there's more to come. After all, business has been very good.

> **LOWELL'S INSIGHT**
>
> **Customer Attention**
> Make sure the customer or tenant is your top priority at all times. Listen to them. Solve their problem. Be bigger than they are. Try not to ever lose a customer or tenant.

"How did we do it?" Lowell asks. "Tell me what changed."

"We got awesome people at properties," comes the response from one long-time employee.

"Teamwork. Everybody is more cohesive," says a regional manager.

"Communication," says another.

All the kinds of answers Lowell likes to hear.

"You don't see me much anymore," he says. "You know why? It's running like a top."

One reason is systems, he adds. "Most successful companies and most successful people have systems." Systems. Reports. Monitoring.

One of his most highly touted business practices that uses a system to produce reports that can be monitored is phone shopping. "It's the biggest reason we blew the doors off the hinges," says Lowell. "We're going to phone shop you. That's running a good company, (making sure we are) taking care of our customers."

With that, he launches into the results of the most recent phone shopping – calls made anonymously to each office at the apartment complexes – to assess how and when the phone is answered and how excited and enthusiastic the employee comes across to the caller. Did the employee ask for the caller's name and number? Did he or she call the person back an hour later? Did the employee discuss the amenities and positive aspects of the apartment complex?

Most performed admirably, scoring an eight or nine out of ten. That wasn't the case in several earlier phone shops. The result, Lowell explains, four people are no longer with the company. They were fired. "We are all over these phone shops. There's nothing more important to our company than that. (Phone shopping) reports are systems. Successful companies have them. Monitor, monitor, monitor. If you want to be successful, have systems and monitor," he tells them again.

Even when he and his family owned numerous funeral homes and cemeteries, they used phone shopping to gauge how well employees were interacting with potential customers. He ranks it near the top of what most companies in most industries should be doing, especially if they deal directly with the public.

Other parts of his talk today reflect his thinking not just on the specifics of the last month and last quarter of the apartment business, but business principles to practice in operating a successful company. Among them: employ the right people – the best jockeys, as he calls them, referring to a strategy of his friend, entrepreneur L. Gale Lemerand, whose book, To Win in Business…Bet on the 'Jockey', highlights the importance Lemerand places on employing the right managers and employees. Business author Jim Collins in his bestselling book, Good to Great: Why Some Companies Make the Leap and Others Don't, found a common thread in his research about companies that made that transition: "…they first got the right people on the bus (and the wrong people off the bus) and then figured out where to drive it."

"You as managers, we're relying on you in hiring the right people," Lowell says. "How much can you change someone? Twenty percent." And, he adds, "The problem is it's (difficult) to hire." Lowell urges them to be smart when they hire.

At times, Lowell has been known to be what he calls a "fire-breathing dragon" when he's upset about someone not performing, or he sees something else that's not right, or is a detriment to the business. A few of the managers have previously seen that side of Lowell. But not today. He does, however, have a few critical comments.

"The biggest mistake now is garbage overflowing (at some apartment complexes). You've got to get better at this. The garbage is driving us crazy. It's unprofessional to have garbage all over the place. No more trash. Concentrate on that more than anything."

One other problem. Next to the mortgage, the single biggest expense for every apartment complex is water, he says. Then he rattles off a few suggestions on how they can make improvements in this area.

Before he concludes his speech, employees see another side of Lowell, a father figure concerned about each one of them as a person. He tells them he wants them to be happy in life. "I can change your life right now! I can change your life today!" he says with the zeal of a preacher handing out hope.

He implores them to stop responding with "good" when someone asks, "How are you?" "When you say 'good,' you just communicated the opposite. You can change that. It's a habit." Say "great" instead of "good."

"I didn't come up with this, but 'good is the enemy of great,'" he says.

He also tells them they shouldn't choose to be around people who are negative. "Spend time with positive people."

"Do random acts of kindness. You will feel one-hundred percent better," he says. For example, thank someone with a five-dollar bill. "You don't have to do it with a hundred-dollar bill."

"As he finishes his speech, he's once again the cheerleader, singing their praises, telling them, "It's so great to have superstars." And then, "You owe it to yourself to be happy the rest of your life."

> ## LOWELL'S INSIGHT
>
> ### Bonuses
> Never forget: nothing will motivate your employees more than team and/or individual bonuses. Normally your sales staff, leasing agents and anyone who communicates with your customers could be awarded. Sometimes include maintenance personnel, office staff and others. It helps create teamwork.
>
> The negative is you must always be aware of expenses. Did the amount you spent on bonuses increase sales enough to offset expenses. Be careful. Do the results merit the cost?

During a short break, Lowell realizes he forgot to recognize and honor the maintenance crews. When the meeting begins again, he points out their accomplishments. "Our expenses are at an all-time low," he says. Then, he gives out four more $100 bills.

To Lowell, today's presentation is about teaching and sharing, quarterbacking and cheerleading. It's who he is. It's part of the game plan he has used in the many businesses he has owned by himself or with family members since the early 1970s. Much of the success, not all of it, but a big portion of it, is measured in the numbers, the dollar values for each business or group of businesses sold: one for $350,000; one for $600,000; a group for $13.5 million; another group for $25 million; and yet another group for $63 million. There are others. A total of more than $110 million. But as spectacular as those numbers are, they are tiny compared with a potential sale Lowell and Ty and Nancy are considering. There are indications a buyer will make a formal offer of $113 million to buy the ten apartment buildings the Lohmans own in Orlando and Jacksonville. But $113 million wouldn't be enough, they say. They were also offered $122 million and turned it down. They're thinking more than $130 million. If a sale does eventually happen, though, Lowell would certainly consider it a crowning achievement, and also an opportunity for more "sharing." At this stage of his life, he still loves making money, and he's still the competitive leader. But business these days serves a larger purpose.

"It's not about how much money you make that is important. It's about how much you give away that really matters," he says. That wasn't always true because he spent decades focused on making more and more money. Recessions in the 1970s affected all businesses, including Lowell's, and prompted him to sell several of his businesses before changing directions and moving into a completely different industry. His finances improved, but it would take a long while before there would be any money to give away even if he wanted to be a philanthropist. When he was growing up, and early in his career, philanthropy wasn't even a word to him. In fact, as a youngster, neither business nor entrepreneurship was a part of his world except for the times he made money as a kid mowing lawns and washing windows. Even in youth, though, he believed himself to be a leader, especially on the football field and baseball diamond. But he had no inkling those leadership skills could be used in real life, in business, to make vast sums of money, and to give a lot of it away.

Chapter 2

Born to Lead

"It is while we are young that the habit of industry is formed. If not then, it never is afterwards. The fortune of our lives, therefore, depends on employing well the short period of youth."

Thomas Jefferson

When Lowell was a youngster, other boys looked up to him and relied on him. He was their pitcher in baseball, their quarterback in football, their captain and leader. Their cheerleader. He felt the responsibility of leadership. And he loved it. The exhilaration he felt when the eyes of ten football players in the huddle were focused on him was like the rush of a runner's high. What would he say? What would he do? How would he make plays?

Even at twelve years old, throwing and catching baseballs with his younger brother, Victor, Lowell relished being the one making the decisions. Some of that, of course, was because that's what older brothers tend to do, especially when there is a six-year age difference. But leadership traits were there, unrefined and perhaps masquerading as an ornery big brother.

"I made him play with me," says Lowell. "He would cry to mother, hollering at her from the back yard because I wouldn't let him quit. He would call to her so that she would come outside and make us stop."

Victor had his own strategies. "In the backyard, Lowell was teaching me how to pitch, and I would get tired and not want to do it anymore. I would throw a wild pitch so he'd have to go chase the ball, and then I would run in the house and start calling for our mother to get him to let me go."

But because of Lowell's insistence, or perhaps in spite of it, Victor helped Lowell become a better athlete, a star pitcher and excellent hitter. He set records in baseball in high school and at Brevard Junior College in Cocoa, Florida. Victor excelled, too. He became a very good athlete who ultimately had a tryout with the farm team of the Los Angeles Dodgers, which held spring training in the Lohman boys' hometown, Vero Beach, Florida. Victor was a stand-out pitcher in high school. An arm injury forced him to rely on his hitting and fielding skills, but those didn't quite match what the Dodgers wanted. Aside from baseball, Victor became an excellent golfer who eventually played a brief stint on the Senior Tour of the Professional Golf Association.

Looking back, Lowell is certain the natural leadership ability honed in his youth, and then polished as he matured, is one of the reasons for his success in business. And, akin to natural leadership or a part of it, Lowell believes he and most successful leaders and business executives possess both power and warmth.

"If you have too much power, but not enough warmth, you will probably be limited as to how far you can take your company or organization. If you have too much warmth, but not enough power, you probably don't need to be in business for yourself."

Lowell didn't have an interest in business growing up

in Vero Beach, or when he went to Brevard Junior College, or to Florida State University. His love of business, indeed a passion for business, didn't come until after he received his college degree, which wasn't in business, but in biology. Neither business nor biology was part of the Lohman household.

Lowell's father, Edgar, was a military man. He enlisted in the U.S. Navy as a young man and spent thirty-seven years in active duty and the reserve. He was stationed at the Naval Air Station in Vero Beach, a training facility where he was a dive bomb squadron flight engineer. In civilian life, he worked thirty-five years for the U.S. Postal Service.

"My relationship with my dad was about as good as you can imagine. He was our biggest cheerleader, my two brothers and me. He was always there, always behind us one-hundred percent," says Lowell.

Lowell's mother, Opal Mae "Ope" Holland, was born and raised in Vero Beach, and it was there she met Edgar. The couple married just before World War II ended and remained in Vero Beach where Lowell was born on February 16, 1945. Six years later, in 1951, Victor was born. And then, six years after that, Daryl, in 1957.

Opal was "tall, dark and elegant," says Lowell. "Everybody, all the time, said if you took one look at her, you'd say, 'Boy, she reminds me of Elizabeth Taylor.' When she walked into a room, it would stop. She was very striking – and I'm not just saying that because she's my mom. She really was."

The Lohman family lived in rental homes until Lowell was about ten. Then they moved to 2244 Bonita Avenue, a small two-bedroom, one-bath house Edgar built. It was just south of the Naval Air Station and not far west of U.S. Highway 1, in McAnsh Park, one of the nicer neighborhoods at that time.

Lowell had lots of buddies there. So, playing baseball and football with the neighborhood boys was a frequent occurrence.

The Lohmans were a typical middle class working family. Edgar supervised the postal service's U.S. Civil Service examinations and related activities in five counties. Opal worked at The Petite Shop, a fashionable clothing store built in 1952 and one of the first retail shops on the beachside in Vero Beach.

Like Edgar, Opal supported her sons' involvement in sports, and she attended many of their games.

Even before Lowell was eight years old and starting to play Little League Baseball and Midget Football, he was a pitcher, at least in his mind. At the family's home on Bonita Avenue, he threw balls against the side of the house. Over and over and over. His arm fared better than the house. A crack developed on one wall.

When he was about eleven or twelve, he noticed a change in his talent and ability. Others saw it, too. Lowell felt like he had developed into the best athlete in his age group. Teammates and coaches realized it, and they looked to him to lead. He embraced the role.

Aside from sports, life revolved around family and church, although Lowell says both his mom and dad were "semi-religious." It was Opal's mother and father, Sarah and Jesse Holland, who were the primary forces for making sure their daughter and grandsons attended church. Sarah also frequently took care of Lowell when Opal was working. Lowell says he "grew up with a lot of religion," and he didn't mind going to church a couple of times a week, usually at the Church of God. But as he got older and enrolled at Florida State University, religion lost its allure as he became more interested in biology and other science topics such as evolution. He stopped going to church.

A few times each year, Lowell's family would travel to Miami to visit Edgar's relatives. Edgar's father was deceased by then, but his mother and several of his brothers were there. For Lowell, it was also a place to throw baseballs and footballs with his cousins, Bobby and Edmund Lohman. "I have great memories of spending time with them," Lowell says.

He learned about work at a relatively young age. At eight or nine years old, he not only mowed the family's lawn, he earned money by cutting grass for others in the neighborhood. "I didn't mind the lawn mowing, but every once in a while, they'd want me to come and weed their flowerbed. I hated doing that." As he got older, his mother got him a job on many Saturday mornings washing windows at The Petite Shop. "It had a lot of windows… It probably took me three or four hours." After he finished, he headed to the nearby beach. He liked earning spending-money, and he didn't begrudge working. "My recollection on all of it is positive. You probably should work at that age."

As a junior in high school, fish changed Lowell's life. Not catching them, but researching a specific fish – the tiny Rivulus marmoratus, also called the Mangrove Rivulus. They "can survive for up to two months in wet leaves, logs, small puddles, and crab burrows, 'breathing' through their skin. They flip head-over-tail across land to travel to better locations," and "they are able to fertilize their own eggs," according to Florida Museum at the University of Florida.

Science was Lowell's favorite subject in junior high and high school, and he especially liked biology because it involved animals, nature and math. Biology can be a difficult subject, but Lowell was a fairly good student, making mostly B's, and he was pretty good with numbers. He landed a summer job to help research the Rivulus Marmoratus at what is known today as Florida Medical Entomological Laboratory, part of the University of Florida's Institute of Food and Agricultural Sciences about three miles south of Vero Beach.

> *LOWELL'S INSIGHT*
>
> **Education**
> It is important to get a college education. Beg, plead, borrow, work, take student loans, etc. In today's world, the price you will pay is even larger, particularly in the business world if you do not have a formal education.

"I will never forget this, and I'm probably sixteen years old. Most of the people working there had their PhD's or at least their Master's. There was a cafeteria where they would all meet. So, I would sit and listen to all of them talk about what they're doing, and it just mesmerized me. I think I liked it anyway, but as soon as that summer started, it influenced me a lot."

Not a glamorous job, he spent a lot of time using a pipette, cleaning up after fish residing in Mason jars. But that, of course, wasn't the part of the job that fascinated him. It was when he and one of the researchers waded into marshes around Vero Beach and used a metal tool to take out a plug of grass and mud where the Rivulus marmoratus sometimes lived. "We went to different areas to see if we could determine where they were concentrated and why they were there versus other areas. We would sample other areas that didn't have any. The whole scenario was interesting."

Lowell was not one of those youngsters who was always getting into trouble. He was usually the boy in the crowd who was the responsible one. But that didn't mean he always did what his parents expected. When he was about fourteen or fifteen, he and a few friends decided to go to the pool hall, which was off limits. As they were shooting pool, Opal appeared at the entrance. Furious, her arms were crossed and squeezed tight in anger. She stared at Lowell. As soon as he saw her, she turned, and she was gone. Lowell told his friends he was in big trouble. "I remember telling them, 'My daddy's gonna wear my ass out.'"

It was the only time Lowell remembers ever getting a spanking, but because he knew it was coming, he decided to see if he could soften the blow. He put a newspaper in the seat of his pants.

Lowell concentrated most of his time, energy and talent on baseball and football, although he also played basketball through his sophomore year in high school. Victor describes Lowell as being a "great athlete" who was probably better in baseball than football, although his quarterbacking skills "stood out tremendously." That included his leadership abilities. "Quarterbacks are traditionally known as being leaders on the team, but it wasn't just from the quarterback position. It was how much his players liked him, and how they listened to him."

Lowell discovered that being quarterback of the football team and captain of the baseball team made him very popular in school, especially with the girls. His dating even earned him a reprieve from some household chores.

"I used to help wash dishes after we ate, and then when I got into high school, and I was out on a date with someone, my fingertips had wrinkles. If you wash dishes a lot, your hands will do that. I remember being on a date one time, and the girl asking me, 'Do you wash dishes? Have you been washing dishes?' I went back and told mother that. I never had to wash another dish."

His excellent plays in baseball, including setting a hitting record when he batted for a .509 average, drew the attention of Brevard Junior College Coach Bob Aiken in Cocoa, Florida, just up the road from Vero Beach. Lowell had talent, but he also had the discipline to put in the hours and hours of practice to get better, to be in the top twenty percent. "For the average person, practices are fine, and you have to do them to improve. But the really great athletes (who) develop themselves are doing over and above that," he says.

During his senior year, Lowell was voted the best athlete in school.

His talent and success were rewarded by a scholarship to attend college and play baseball for Coach Aiken after graduation from high school in 1963. He was looking forward to playing baseball on another level. He really had no idea what he would study, no one to help him figure it out, and limited financial ability. Lowell would be the first in his immediate family to go to college.

"I had sports mentors, but none regarding education to lead me." In junior college, though, he could take the basics and figure out a major later. So that's what he did. In the back of his mind, he thought of the only subject that held any interest. That was biology.

Lowell had a baseball scholarship, but he also needed to earn money. He didn't find any biology-related jobs, but he did find a summer job at Sears, Roebuck and Company selling suits, socks and other items in the Men's Department. Looking back, he says it was a good fit. "I have a fairly outgoing personality, so I enjoyed it." It was his first job in sales if he didn't count the time he spent rounding up customers for his lawn-mowing business.

He also met a woman, an athlete who was a very good tennis player, although she wasn't at the college, or even in Cocoa. Tina Huggins worked at the YMCA in Fort Pierce, which is between Cocoa and Vero Beach. She was in administration, overseeing many of the YMCA sports. It wasn't long before Tina and Lowell were dating exclusively. Things weren't as good back in the Lohman home in Vero Beach. There was some strain between Edgar and Opal, and it seemed to Lowell it was increasing.

On the college baseball diamond, Lowell excelled as a pitcher and a hitter – and as a leader. But suddenly, it seemed, his health had begun to deteriorate. For thirty days or so, he had been losing weight. Plus, he was always thirsty despite consuming lots of cold drinks. After a visit to the doctor, he was sent to the hospital. The diagnosis: Type 1 diabetes.

LOWELL'S INSIGHT

Health
There is absolutely nothing more important than your health. No matter how successful or happy you are, that will all change if you have an illness and your health deteriorates.

This wasn't the first time he faced a significant health issue. In 1950 when he was only five years old, he contracted the polio virus, a "crippling and potentially deadly infectious disease," according to the Centers for Disease Control and Prevention. In the early 1950s, before polio vaccines became available in 1955, polio outbreaks caused more than fifteen thousand cases of paralysis each year in the United States. Edgar and Opal took their young son to a hospital in Palm

Beach, Florida where his treatment was paid for by the March of Dimes. Lowell was lucky. He recovered with no long-lasting effects. Polio had not affected his ability to run.

Fifteen years later, in college, this stout young man, a seemingly invincible athlete full of life and ambition was now face-to-face with this new menacing health opponent, diabetes. Lowell wasn't going to be able to power through this, no matter how strong-willed he was. There was no cure. All he could do was accept it and adapt to it, for the short term and long term. A change in diet and poking himself with a needle twice a day to inject insulin would become routine. Still, he felt certain the diagnosis wouldn't derail his baseball plans. He was confident that even if he couldn't overcome it, he could at least manage it. It would take some time to learn and adjust to diabetes, which he would have to live with for the rest of his life.

Soon, he was back on the mound, pitching better than ever. He set a school record for strikeouts – nineteen in one game. He also was a good hitter, batting over .350. Talking about it today, Lowell says, "I think all of that goes back to having a younger brother to play with."

Teammates elected him captain and he was named the Most Valuable Player.

With a good arm and excellent eye-hand coordination, Lowell felt confident he could play at the next level, at a university, and perhaps ultimately, even beyond. After two years at Brevard, he decided to attend Florida State University in Tallahassee because "it was the best baseball school in the Southeast. At that point, everybody was saying 'You are going to be playing professional baseball.'"

In 1966, he and two of his teammates, a catcher and a reliever, all headed to FSU. None of them were offered a baseball scholarship. All they had were desire and confidence. If only that were enough to pay the tuition, the rent and the grocery bills. And if only the curveballs in life wouldn't be so unhittable.

Chapter 3

Life Detour

"It is difficulties which show what men are."
Epictetus

Baseball practice at FSU wouldn't start until spring. But several months before that, around Christmas time as Lowell was settling in at the university as a member of the Phi Delta Theta fraternity, he had another important matter to attend to. And it was big. Life-changing, in fact.

He learns he's going to be a father. Tina is pregnant.

"I'm sitting there saying, OK, what's the most important thing?" he recalls.

He knew the answer. And he knew life would forever be different.

Dreams of baseball and college suddenly seemed like paper airplanes on a windy day.

Soon, he and Tina married in Pensacola where her parents lived. On May 16, 1967, their son, Brian, was born.

The joy of parents with a newborn crashed into the reality of the young couple struggling financially, trying to provide for themselves and their child. Lowell was trying to figure out how he could continue classes at FSU and whether he would be able to play baseball.

"My life got turned upside down," he recalls. "I think I felt huge pressure."

> **LOWELL'S INSIGHT**
>
> **Adapt**
> Change what you can. Accept what you can't change.

As much as it hurt, and it hurt a lot, Lowell realized a potential career in baseball took second place to providing and caring for family and handling his diabetes. So, baseball was out. The hurt didn't go away as quickly. The pain of not being out there with his buddies as he watched while sitting in the stands struck him like a ninety mile-per-hour fastball.

Not knowing what might have been, whether he was good enough to make it at the university level and even in the big leagues is one of his biggest regrets. He was certainly confident enough. But that didn't matter.

Paying for college was a challenge, but that started from the very first day he arrived at FSU. He recalls pondering the enormity of the situation as he thought about his paltry sum of funds. "I remember at the fraternity, sitting on the back steps one time, when I really looked at it, there was a question of whether I would make it or not."

He had to figure out how to make it on his own because his family wasn't in a position to provide much help beyond encouragement. Also, Edgar and Opal were still dealing with the growing storm in their marriage, which would soon end in divorce. Lowell had seen it coming, but it was still tough for him to accept.

Lowell found two jobs – at a convenience store where he worked as a clerk, and later at a car rental agency. "I worked at the convenience store because you could work one of two shifts, from 7 a.m. to 3 p.m., or you could come in at 3 and work until 11 p.m. The good news about that is I figured out a way to work and continue to take classes…. I worked at the convenience store at nights, then later at the Tallahassee Airport car rental at night, and still took the minimum class-load, which was twelve hours. But I actually, for one or two terms, didn't enroll at all."

The young couple struggled, but they were getting by. Lowell was the only one of them enrolled at FSU, and his courses proved to be formidable. Because he was still uncertain about what to study when he arrived at FSU, he chose the only subject that held any previous interest: biology. "I had a year of genetics, physics, chemistry – and if you major in biology, you get all the rest. I didn't know until I got to Florida State that biology is one of the hardest majors on the planet."

> *LOWELL'S INSIGHT*
>
> **Study Business**
> If you are not sure what to major in, choose business. With a business degree, your options are unlimited. So many young people select a major that after graduation can't provide them with a job or doesn't provide them with the tools to start their own business.

He learned a valuable lesson from his decision. It's one he passes along to all young people who haven't settled on what they will study when they enter college. "If you're unsure, major in business." It opens up many options, he says, because the fundamentals in business are the same in all businesses. "I wish I had had somebody direct me a little bit better."

Working at the car rental agency, Lowell met many

business executives. One of them was Forbes Davis, who lived in Sarasota, Florida, but frequently flew into Tallahassee and rented a car to drive to one of his company's locations in nearby Thomasville, Georgia. The company Forbes and several of his family members owned was Davis Industries, which was in the business of building water and sewer treatment plants, and manufacturing water meters. Most of the work served engineers and developers who were building residential subdivisions outside the reach of municipal utilities.

During a period of about six months, Lowell and Forbes got to know each other relatively well. Forbes determined this young man had potential beyond renting cars. It was fortuitous for Lowell because he was nearing graduation in 1969 following three years of classes instead of the two normally needed after attending a junior college for two years. He was thinking he might get a job as a high school biology teacher and coach.

"As soon as Forbes found out I was a biology major, and I think he knew my personality, he realized that with my background I could work and deal with engineers and developers. So we started talking." Sure enough, Forbes offered Lowell a job. "He threw a figure out at me and I almost fell over. I forget what it was now, but I can remember my reaction." It was far more money that Lowell had ever made.

The job was in sales working out of the Davis Industries Sarasota office. Lowell would be a sales engineer, which meant he would be working with the company's distributors and with project engineers to win business from developers who needed new water and treatment facilities and ongoing laboratory testing. All that biology work that so taxed Lowell would finally pay off. The job seemed like a good fit for Lowell to use his limited sales experience and his new science expertise. Lowell was excited and also glad he had decided against pursuing a job teaching high school biology and coaching baseball and football. Before he met Forbes, Lowell explored the teaching-coaching idea in Fort Myers, Florida, at the urging of a friend who was a head coach at one of the high schools there. But as much as Lowell's life had revolved around sports, this did not seem like a viable career path. "Everyone I talked to said, 'You'll enjoy it, but you won't make any money. It's a nice profession and a nice living.' What my brain said was 'I don't have to be a school teacher to coach....' I said I could coach American Legion baseball, I could coach Little League baseball, I could coach Midget football. So, I said, 'Don't let it influence you that the only way you can coach, which I really enjoyed, is if you're a teacher.' It isn't true."

Playing baseball and football always boosted Lowell's self-confidence, but it rose to another level when he received his diploma – the first person Lowell knew of in his family to earn a college degree. "It's amazing how that piece of paper takes you in a different direction.... amazing what that little piece of paper can do. It doesn't mean you're smarter. What a college degree means is you're more dedicated because it's not easy getting through those four or five years if you don't have any money.... Leadership from sports teams is one thing, but there's not anybody, from doctors to lawyers, that I could look in the eye, and feel inferior to. For people that don't have that piece of paper, it hurts them."

Edgar and Opal and Irv all attended Lowell's graduation ceremony. Edgar and Opal had divorced, and she and Irv Silverman married. Lowell remembered the first time he met Irv during an earlier trip home to Vero Beach from Tallahassee. Opal, Irv, Victor and Lowell had lunch in one of the nicest restaurants in Vero Beach.

"I remember the feelings I had. I remember how nervous Irv and mother were because they had Victor and Daryl, but here comes the college kid. I remember the reaction because I saw Irv in a similar situation – he was divorced and had three kids," says Lowell. "I was happy because I could tell how much he loved mother. He had the ability to give her the finer things in life. She was in love. I was happy for her; I was sad for daddy. I wished they had stayed together, no question. My dad just had a heart of gold; you could count on him. There's nothing negative about daddy, but Irv provided her with an amazing lifestyle."

Irv also was a positive influence on Lowell, who had no idea at the time the role Irv would eventually have in Lowell's life. On college graduation day, though, Lowell was thinking about the immediate future and feeling immense relief that he had overcome the struggles to earn a degree. "It was the biggest accomplishment of my life, so far."

He also believed in the future for him and his young family as he and Tina and Brian prepared to move to Sarasota. It was much, much more than the start of a new job or the start of a career. It would be a foray into business and the opening of a world of opportunities for a twenty-four-year-old young man filled with ambition.

Chapter 4

Calculated Risks

"In the choice of your profession or your business employment, let your first thought be: Where can I fit in so that I may be most effective in the work of the world? Where can I lend a hand in a way most effective to advance the general interests? Enter life in such a spirit, choose your vocation in that way, and you have taken the first step on the highest road to a large success."
John D. Rockefeller

At Davis Industries, Lowell's title was sales engineer, a salesman who was only one member of a team rather than being in his familiar roles of leader and quarterback. It still seemed like a perfect job.

"I loved it. It's exciting, and I'm making good money," he recalls. "I hadn't ever been in real sales, but I think everything we all do is related to sales, to some degree. I knew I had a nice personality. I felt like I was a nice person. I knew I had the educational background. I thought I was a good salesman, too."

His job was working with engineers and independently owned distributors – and calling on developers of residential subdivisions to sell them on having Davis Industries build their water and sewer treatment plants. "Probably the part I enjoyed the most, and the one I concentrated on, was the developers. The good thing was, I was dealing with people who had their own businesses."

He paid close attention to how developers and others operated their businesses, trying to learn and understand as much as he could about these entrepreneurs and what made them successful. Deep down inside, he had a desire to be like them, a business owner rather than an employee.

One part of Lowell's sales strategy, which he would ultimately use for decades, was to take a prospect to lunch because he felt it gave him a better opportunity to get to know the person and to make a favorable impression. Plus, he believed it gave him a slight advantage over his competitors. Sometimes he would convince the prospect to play golf, yet another way to build a relationship that could lead to a sale. "It's not complicated. If the person likes you, there's a good chance you're going to get the job," he says.

> *LOWELL'S INSIGHT*
>
> **Rejection in Sales**
> You have to understand that it's a numbers game. You have to teach salespeople to not take it personally. If you take things personal, you don't ever need to be in sales because rejection is part of the game. Sales is not for everybody.

Of course, persistence is also a necessary component in sales. Lowell believed many of his competitors weren't making the repeat visits to a prospect if they didn't make the sale initially. He did. "If you go back a second time and you don't get the sale, no big deal. They're used to people calling on them all the time. You go back the third time, it's different, and they know you're stable, they can lean on you. They knew I knew more about those treatment plants than they did. So, they had to rely on me. I made sure I was always there."

Having competitors simply upped the ante for Lowell. "It made me hustle more."

His go-getter attitude, competitiveness and leadership skills made an early impression on his bosses. Within about three months, he was named sales manager overseeing six distributorships in Florida. And, even though he himself had received limited training in sales, he was soon the one conducting sales training. His job also meant traveling the state of Florida from Tallahassee to Key West to work with engineers and distributors, and calling on developers.

In his personal life, Lowell had become more contented with family and fatherhood, in part because the financial pressure on him had eased compared with his time in college.

"I had money, and life was good."

He and Tina bought a house near a golf course in Sarasota, and they had a second son, Ty Gene Lohman, who was born February 5, 1971.

Although Lowell spent a lot of time working, he was still an athlete at heart and not one to watch from the sidelines. He participated. He played flag football, which he had started playing at FSU not long after he arrived. Flag football teams are in many cities and often a part of the U.S. Flag & Touch Football League.

After about three years at Davis Industries, Lowell saw an opportunity to go into business for himself. Not solely, but with a partner. Still, it was his entry into business as an entrepreneur. His partner's name was Carl Ashton, who was in Fort Pierce, just up the road from Lowell's hometown of Vero

Beach. Carl was one of the independent distributors for Davis Industries – and one of the people Lowell called on and worked with in his job as sales manager.

The idea behind the partnership was that Lowell could help Carl increase his business because Lowell would handle sales, calling on developers of subdivisions. After a sale, Carl would build the water and treatment plants. Carl also owned a utility company installing water and sewer lines, and a side business installing septic tanks. Lowell wasn't going to be involved in those parts of the business. However, he saw another opportunity for the pair. Lowell believed Carl was missing out on a continual revenue stream because he did not own a laboratory to handle the required monthly testing of water and sewage at the treatment plants he was building. So, the young man with the biology and science background, and now sales experience, convinced Carl they should build and operate a laboratory.

The partnership was equal, fifty-fifty. Lowell had to come up with money for his part – and he did that by selling his house in Sarasota. He and Tina had built up some equity – and that would turn into the cash he needed to go into business with Carl. Tina didn't object, and Lowell didn't hesitate. Selling a house or taking a second mortgage are among the ways many entrepreneurs get their start. It's a method Lowell still believes in.

"There's always risk when you go into business for yourself. I didn't think it was a risk. It came more from confidence, and I already had the contacts in this business. I had spent a lot of money taking people to lunch," says Lowell. "I (also) think part of it was I wanted to be back in Vero. I think inside of me, I kept observing. I was like a sponge when I got into the real business world. I just knew I could do it. I knew if I sold my house, I'd have a little bit of money to contribute. I knew I had the college education, and that I was a hard worker. I knew I had the drive."

His motivation stemmed more from an innate desire to succeed than from the idea that he was going into business to make a million dollars, or millions of dollars.

"I don't think the money was the driving force. Of course, it's easy to say that when you have the money, but you have to go back and analyze that. I just wanted to be in business for myself. There was something inside of me that wanted to prove that I could do it, and do a great job with it."

Lowell left his job with Davis Industries and the young family moved to Vero Beach. He and his partner would concentrate their efforts in a one-hundred-fifty-mile stretch of Florida's east coast from Vero Beach north into Brevard County and south to Palm Beach County.

Within about six months, Lowell and Carl were getting their share of the business from developers. Their company, Indian River Utilities, also contracted to handle testing for others who didn't have that capability. And, of course, for the water and treatment facilities Carl and Lowell built and operated, they did the testing. "I had two guys that would, once a week, go to the treatment plants to make sure they were working right. Then once a month, we had to do the lab work and send it to Tallahassee, to the Department of Environmental Regulation."

Although business was good, Lowell had been seduced by the entrepreneurial life. He was always on the lookout for the next opportunity. He found it at the Lamplighter Mobile Home Park in Sebastian, just north of Vero Beach.

Through servicing the park's treatment plant, Lowell

began to know the owner of the park where there were eighty to ninety mobile homes. The park owned the land and the mobile home owners paid monthly rent for their space. When the park owner mentioned he was thinking about retiring, Lowell offered to buy the place. He didn't have the money, but he took a second mortgage on the house he and Tina had purchased in Vero Beach. They had rented when they first moved there – actually rented the house he grew up in – but they did eventually buy a house on the beachside off State Road A1A. So, once again, Lowell and Tina's home was the piggy bank for a new business. Of course, Lowell also had been building relationships with bankers because he realized early on that for anyone going into business, finding and getting to know bankers was essential. At this point, it would take $200,000 to buy the park from the owner, who offered to finance it for Lowell.

> ## *LOWELL'S INSIGHT*
>
> ### Entrepreneurship
>
> If you have the entrepreneurial spirit, choose an industry you have an interest in. Go to work for the best company in that industry and learn while getting paid. Concentrate and learn every aspect of the business: marketing, finance, banking, competition, networking, sales, etc.
>
> At some point, you may say to yourself, 'I'm ready.' Remember, every business has a moment. Do you have enough cash? Have you established banking relationships? Should you take a partner? Do you have a relationship with suppliers? Is your confidence level high?

It was Lowell's first business venture on his own. It only whet his appetite.

Soon he found another opportunity – this one in raw land. He teamed up with his stepfather, Irv, to buy approximately ten acres, which they intended to develop as a subdivision filled with homes. It was called Seminole Shores, on the beachside in Vero Beach, fronting State Road A1A and within walking distance to the Atlantic Ocean. They built and paved roads, installed the water and sewer treatment facilities and contracted with one of Lowell's uncles, Jim Odom, who began building houses there, including one for Lowell and Tina. Neither Irv nor Lowell had any experience as developers, but as businessmen, they believed they could figure it out. It turned out to be a steep learning curve for the pair. That didn't slow them down, but there was a coming storm that would.

> ## LOWELL'S INSIGHT
>
> ### Establish Relationships with Bankers
> You cannot create wealth without debt. There are exceptions to that because there are a lot of successful people who don't want to borrow anything. However, growth will be very slow. Anytime an opportunity comes up, you have to have set that groundwork up with your bankers.
>
> Do not have just one banker. If he or she knows they are the only banker you're going to, guess what could happen? They may charge you more interest and may put conditions on you such as requiring you to sign personally. Tell him or her you're accepting competitive bids. You'll be shocked how quickly they will lower their rate. Seventy five percent of people going into business don't know this.

Lowell was still partners with Carl in the utilities and laboratory business, but he wanted to focus on his other businesses. So, he talked with Carl about ending their partnership. A deal was struck. They each took a portion of the service area. No money was exchanged. Lowell also turned over his part of the lab ownership to Carl. For the portion of the business that maintained the water and sewer facilities, Lowell sold that to another businessman for about $350,000. Lowell and Carl parted as friends. Their business had been a success for both of them. Three decades later, Lowell still recalls how it was such a good partnership, which is not always the case when two or more people go into business together.

> ## LOWELLISM
>
> **Partnerships**
> There are three reasons to take a partner in your business. The first is if you don't have the cash and you need an investor. The second is if you need someone who understands the business better than you, and is a hard worker. The third reason is family. In business, I was happiest when I was working with family.

"I can't think of a better business partner you could have had. He let me do everything. He didn't question anything." The two might not have agreed on everything, but they never quarreled about any aspect of the business. Each had his own expertise and responsibilities: Lowell's was sales and getting the business. Carl's was building the treatment facilities.

"If I had to rely on myself for the water and sewage treatment plants, it probably wouldn't have worked," says Lowell. "I never worried about any of it. Carl did a phenomenal job, and he had other projects he was involved with, too, just like I did when I bought the mobile home park and the subdivision."

Throughout much of the 1970s and into the early 1980s, turbulent economic times rocked the United States – and other countries, too. Lingering effects of the 1973 oil crisis, the recession from 1973 to 1975 and another recession beginning in 1980 created wave after wave after wave of challenges and hardships. At various times, and even simultaneously, low economic growth, high unemployment and high rates of inflation took a toll on families, workers and companies. Lowell felt it in his businesses – not early on, but gradually, like a tsunami gathering speed. So much so, that after weathering the storm for a while and taking on unwanted debt, he and Irv decided it was probably the right time to sell the subdivision, which they were still developing. Most homebuyers were having difficulty getting financing, and even if they could, their mortgage rates were sometimes astronomical. So, a deal was reached to sell the subdivision for about $600,000.

> *LOWELL'S INSIGHT*
>
> **Do It Now**
> The average person has no sense of urgency. Successful people have a sense of urgency.

Although Lowell still had monthly rental income from mobile home owners in his park, the economy severely hampered the ability of others to get financing to purchase a mobile home.

Clearly, times were tough. Business wasn't good for entrepreneurs like Lowell or for big companies and corporations.

As family members are inclined to do when many people in the nation are struggling financially, they discuss, cuss and lament the economy and its effects on their own lives and businesses. That's exactly what happened when Lowell and his brother, Victor, and Opal and Irv were together in Vero Beach to celebrate the holidays. They didn't dwell on the difficulties, though. They discussed a new way forward.

Irv posed a suggestion and question to Lowell: Why don't you go to Cocoa and work in pre-need sales at Florida Memorial Gardens Cemetery? Victor was already working there, selling burial spaces. Irv had previously owned that cemetery before selling it to his sales manager, Gene Crow. It was one of a number of cemeteries Irv had owned in Florida. But he had sold all of them and was now retired. Retirement, though, wasn't a great fit for Irv.

For Lowell, pre-need sales – selling cemetery property and merchandise – would mean working for someone else again. But unlike the burial space he would be selling, he wasn't planning on the job being permanent. It was an opportunity, though. He was especially thrilled that the cemetery business would likely be much more resistant to recessions and sour economies than his own businesses had been. People die whether times are good or bad. So, he decided this was too good of an opportunity to pass up.

He eventually put the mobile home park on the market, and sold it for about $450,000. After that, he was no longer a business owner. But in his heart, he was still an entrepreneur.

Chapter 5

'If You Can't Close, You Can't Sell'

"The best salespeople are simply those who understand that there is little difference between obstacles and opportunities and are able to turn both to their advantage."
Victor Kiam, American businessman and entrepreneur

Just as Lowell had done when he was a youngster, he relied on his younger brother, Victor, to help him. But unlike their days when Lowell forced Victor to play catch so the big brother could improve his baseball skills, the two boys now were men working together. And it was Victor who was the teacher. He had the pre-need sales knowledge and experience that could benefit Lowell and help him understand the business. Plus, Victor was doing well and making good money. And that's what the older brother wanted, too.

Victor was uncertain if this would be the job for Lowell because previously he was dealing mostly with other entrepreneurs in business-to-business sales as opposed to selling to couples and individuals ranging in age from mid-twenties to seventies.

"I wasn't sure if that fit Lowell's personality with him going to families' homes. He's obviously a very personable, likeable guy, but I just wasn't sure after owning his own business that it fit into what he was set up to do. However, within three months, I knew immediately that it was perfect for him.... It surprised me that he took off pretty quick with it."

Lowell wouldn't be Lowell if he didn't put his all into it, and as he likes to say, "attack" the job. He wasn't the boss or owner, but he certainly had a burning desire to learn – and to be the best he could be.

The two salesmen, along with several others, didn't usually have to search for prospects. Some people would call to make inquiries about a cemetery space. Others mailed in a coupon for a special offer. It was then up to the pre-need counselors as they were known, to make the sale. The cemetery also employed telemarketers, and they generated leads. Calls would be placed to a family with the offer for one free burial space in the cemetery, worth about three-hundred dollars at that time. An appointment would be set so the sales counselor could meet with the family and deliver the certificate for the space.

"Everyone's response was, 'OK, what's the catch? You're not really giving me a cemetery space.' There really is no catch, but there's a reason," says Lowell. "Once you explain it to people, we know if we give them a space, they're probably going to buy another one."

Lowell had considerable experience in sales when he started in the cemetery industry. He always believed he was a born salesman. This new job seemed ideal because it allowed him to use his sales skills and people skills, and he was quickly convinced of the merits of what he was selling. He believed individuals and families should plan ahead and purchase their cemetery spaces, cemetery memorialization and funeral services.

"I loved the job," he says. "I liked that you had some flexibility, and I liked talking to people. I still do. The people we were talking to were a little bit older and they needed the product, I believe. Still do. If you do it ahead of time, you save so much money, and your family doesn't have to go through all the financial decisions on one of the worst days of their lives. It doesn't take long to figure that out. Anyone that's seventy- to eighty-years-old who hasn't done anything, shame on them because they're going to leave it to their families with no instructions and the difficulty, for some, to pay for it."

LOWELLISM

Work Together
The worst word is 'I'. The best word is 'We'.

From the start, Lowell began keeping a diary, writing in an eight-by-ten black notebook with Record written on the cover. He listed lessons he learned and sales strategies and systems he could use. Most of what he wrote could be applied to many types of selling regardless of the product or service.

Excerpts from Lowell's Writings in the 1970s
Lowell's Sales Tips

If someone has shown an interest in cemetery property by answering an ad or mailing in a coupon, they should NEVER be contacted by telephone in an attempt to set an appointment. The counselor should go to the prospect's house as soon as possible, preferably driving the evening of or on week-ends when the probability of both members being home is greatest.

Once an appointment with a prospect has been set, every attempt must be made to run the appointment on time. Anytime the counselor contacts the prospect to reset or change the time, the chances are great that he may lose the prospect completely. However, if an appointment change is unavoidable, the counselor should always notify the prospect in an attempt to set another time.

When attempting to set an appointment time with a prospect, do not ask if a specific time is convenient. Instead give them a choice of at least two different times. Example: If you ask Mr. Jones if Saturday at 1:00 is convenient, you will receive either a yes or no answer. However, if you ask Mr. Jones would 1:00 or 4:00 be more convenient, you will receive either a 1:00 or 4:00.

LOWELLISM

Work
Successful people do the things unsuccessful people are not willing to do.

When approaching a prospects home, the counselor should always pull in the drive, not park on the street. A quick check should be made prior to arrive to assure that all materials needed for a presentation and contract signing are in order. Once in the drive, the counselor should not hesitate, but should walk briskly to the door.

Do not ring the doorbell! Most people associate the ring of a doorbell with strangers, whereas a firm knock normally denotes a friend.

If a family is not home, the counselor should go to a telephone and call. They may be resting or not hear you knock.

If you are late for an appointment by 30 minutes or less, run the appointment anyway. If you are 45 minutes or more, late, call them.

Once inside the prospects home, the counselor should divorce himself from his kit immediately.

Anytime only one member of the family is home, it is fruitless to give a presentation. Their standard reply at the end of a presentation will be they will check with their spouse and let you know. You should inform them that this is the type of thing that both members should be together and set a definite time to meet again either at their home or at the cemetery.

Once inside the home, the first few minutes of the warm up are crucial. The counselor should be complimentary and look for clues to the prospects' interests such as plants, animals, trophies, etc. The initial conversation should not be about cemetery property but rather items of interest to the prospect.

Upon entering the home, the counselor should usually locate a table which will be used after the warm-up to present the counselor's program.

After the warm-up, the counselor should use physical action to get the family to the table. This is done by rising and as you walk toward the table, telling the family you can better explain the program at the table.

Without a doubt, the positioning of individuals at the table can determine whether the sale is obtained or lost. The counselor should take control at this point to be sure he is seated facing both members of the family. If a counselor is seated between prospects, all it takes is a negative nod from one to the other when the counselor least expects it and the sale is lost. Do not be timid when placing members of the family.

You must have a family's complete attention if a sale is to be made. If the T.V. is too loud, you can talk softly so that it is difficult to hear, (and) they will normally turn the T.V. off at this point. If this does not work, do not hesitate to go to the T.V. and ask if you can turn it off.

When referring to finance charges, do not use the words, interest or finance. A better word would be carrying charges.

When signing a contract, do not use words such as sign here. It is better to ask them to O.K. the agreement. Avoid referring to the contract as a contract. Agreement is a better word.

The three-day notice of cancellation should be explained early in the list of paperwork to be completed. It should never be the last item explained. It should be referred to as a Right of Recision, not a Notice of Cancellation.

In explaining the program and cost, one should always print and never write longhand. Each point should be distinct and easily read. A dark felt tip pen should be used. Never use red.

If the counselor takes a short rest in the afternoon prior to running his appointments, he will be refreshed and energetic while the prospect will be tired and not as willing to resist.

FEAR – Is the uncertainty about the reception we will receive at the prospect's door. Our fears are grossly exaggerated.

Most prospects toss out an objection to slow the counselor's advance, not caring that it may not be honest. The counselor should acknowledge it and then ignore it.

Experience shows that most families who own property located some distance from the city in which they live will buy locally when death strikes.

On a free space program where the family has 15 days to select their space, the counselor should contact the family several days prior to their deadline to set an appointment.

This is one of the very few occupations where you are actually in business for yourself.

Additional Excerpts
FEAR

Short Nap Refreshes The Counselor.

FEAR – Is Being Afraid of the Reception We Will Receive At The Door.

HABIT Is The Counselor's Greatest Asset.

Must Establish Control Of Presentation – Don't let Prospect Control You.

Don't Make A Sales Talk With A 3rd Party Looking On.

If You Cannot Receive Their Undivided Attention – Leave!

Counselors Should Develop Their Talents As Interesting Individuals.

People Buy Because They Learn To Like The Counselor.

Within twelve to eighteen months after Lowell had begun his pre-need sales job, a new opportunity opened up. Neither he nor Victor remembers whether they found a cemetery in Ormond Beach, Florida they might be able to buy, or whether Irv found it. Either way, to all of them, this seemed like an ideal situation to become owners.

"We really hadn't thought of buying multiple locations. We just said here's one for Victor and Lowell to run," says Victor. "We were moving to the next phase where we were the bosses."

The cemetery was Ormond Memorial Park, a small place, about thirty acres, and there was no funeral home on the property. It was in receivership and state administrators were anxious to find a new owner. The two Lohman brothers and their mother and Irv purchased it together. They negotiated one hundred percent bank financing.

Lowell and Victor moved to Ormond Beach so they could manage the property – and of course, handle pre-need sales, which is the lifeblood of a cemetery. Without a strong pre-need sales program, it's not good business. It's simply not financially feasible to wait until the time of need to sell burial space or related items and services.

They changed the name to Volusia Memorial Park to reflect the name of the county and they began their sales push. It worked.

"I remember the first year we doubled the sales compared to what had ever been done in the past for that cemetery," Victor says. "We went to Irv, saying we doubled the sales, and he told us to double that again before it would impress him. We busted our butts to double it again, and we did, and that's when we just realized we were both into it and we were both good at it."

Within a couple of years, Irv's connections from having previously owned a number of cemeteries paid off. He heard about a cemetery in Ocala, Florida, about seventy miles west of Ormond Beach, that was having problems. The owner was looking to sell.

> ## LOWELL'S INSIGHT
>
> **Managing**
> Take your key people to lunch as often as you can. It gets them out of the office, and you can personally train them and get to know them better. It shows you care. I can get more training done over lunch with them than I can back in the office.

"We were interested," says Victor. "We talked with the gentleman and while we were there he mentioned that he had another one in Eustis, Florida. I just remember (sitting) on the hood of the car talking to him, and all of sudden, next thing we know, we're buying a cemetery in Eustis we've never seen before. We're adding that to the contract."

They decided Victor would oversee the cemeteries in Ormond Beach and Eustis. Lowell would be in charge of the property in Ocala, spending two to three days a week there. The remainder of the time, he would be in Ormond Beach focusing on pre-need sales.

The business worked well with the brothers being equal in position, although Victor had more years of experience. The two of them enjoyed working together. Of course, they didn't always agree on everything. "That's normal for brothers and families involved together in business," says Victor. None of the disagreements threatened their relationship as business owners or brothers. There also were no issues with their mother and Irv being a part of the business, although neither of them was involved in the day-to-day operations. They still lived in Vero Beach. "Irv would come up a lot more in the beginning, more like once a month, and then it turned into once every three months," says Victor. "That was mainly because our mother wanted to see us. It was a very close family."

It seemed only natural that the family would decide to get into the funeral home business. None of them had that kind of experience, but they knew it would be enormously beneficial to have cemeteries and funeral homes, especially if they were located together. The state of Florida had long prohibited that. But no longer. The first funeral home the Lohman brothers and their mother and Irv bought, however, did not have a cemetery, but it would be a start in the funeral business. It was in South Daytona, which is near Ormond Beach. They remodeled it and operated it. After they learned the business, they built a funeral home next to the first cemetery they purchased. That new facility would be called Volusia Funeral Home.

Ironically, neither Victor nor Lowell wanted to become a funeral director. They preferred to hire licensed funeral directors. Lowell's interest was pre-need sales and overall business operation and growth. Victor's preference was pre-need sales and cemetery operations, although now as one of the owners of the funeral homes, he found out he had to learn about the various roles of funeral directors, including their job of preparing bodies for funerals and burials.

> **LOWELL'S INSIGHT**
>
> **Attorneys and Accountants**
> Selecting the right attorney and accountant are probably the most important decisions you will make in the business world. If possible, try to select people who have experience in your industry. Make sure your personalities are similar and that they understand your personality. They should become your friend and advisor. Always consult with them before finalizing a transaction. Then make your best business decision.

"I just never wanted to go into the prep room," says Victor. "I didn't think that was the place for me. I remember when we were building the funeral home, all of a sudden, our funeral directors are coming to me with their tools and equipment they need, and they handed me a bill that was extremely high. It was shocking. I decided I didn't want to hear any more and just signed the check. That was a little more in-depth from the funeral directors' side that I didn't want to know."

Lowell and Victor's brother, Daryl, who is six years younger than Victor, also came into the family business. During the summer before his final year at Florida State University, he came to Ormond Beach to work in pre-need sales at the cemetery. He said with a laugh that he "was kind of thrown out into the field to prove my worth," although the brothers did provide sales training. After graduating with a business degree in 1980, he was back in Ormond Beach within a week, this time to work full time in the family business. Lowell says, "I was so proud of Daryl for graduating from college, particularly as a Florida State

Seminole."

The family purchased a cemetery in Winter Haven, (Florida), and as Victor recalls, Daryl joked that 'you guys just kicked me out and shuffled me over to Winter Haven.' Daryl managed both the sales and operation of the Winter Haven property for nearly ten years. "He did a phenomenal job," says Victor. During that time, Daryl oversaw the addition of a new funeral home at the cemetery.

Daryl loved the job and he was thrilled to be a part of the family business. He knew, even when he was in college, that he was destined to work with the family. And, like his brothers, he was a good salesman. "I did real well," he says, and although he was the youngest and the last to enter the business, he was an equal partner. "We never had different titles. We were all vice presidents." Lowell says Daryl was "the best pre-need sales manager" he had ever seen.

The family formed a company they called Sloman – a play on Irv's last name, Silverman, combined with the Lohman name. Each of the five partners owned twenty percent of the company.

They were flying high with confidence, partly because sales were good and business was good. They believed they knew what they were doing and they felt they understood both the cemetery business and the funeral home business, what worked and what didn't work.

They continued to add Florida cemeteries and funeral homes to their holdings. Locations included Jacksonville, Lakeland and Orlando. They built additional funeral homes in Ocala and Lakeland. They also bought a company that made and sold the vaults used in cemetery spaces.

They all liked the fact their company was expanding.

Somewhat remarkably, they worked together very well when one considers there was no formal chain of command and no CEO who could have the last word or make final decisions. Each of the five family members was an equal partner.

All three of the brothers were competitive, Type A personalities, and so too were Irv and Opal. Many family-owned businesses struggle because individuals can't seem to work together, or even if they do, there are underlying tensions that can easily lead to disasters, ongoing crises or business failure. Why did it all work so well with the Lohman family?

"We were one of the very fortunate families," says Victor. "Our mother loved us to death and we loved our mom. So, she was the one who, if she saw fireworks, she would step in. Irv was very low key and very business-minded. Then you have Victor, Lowell and Daryl. We were sports-minded and competitive. Day-to-day it was great... I think the business was good for us. We are very outgoing people. So, for the sales end of the business, it was a natural.... Once or twice during the year, we might not have a good day, but you have that just being brothers. From a business standpoint, we saw that we were doing positive things. We all knew what our goals were – increasing sales and growing our businesses."

"We really had good dynamics," says Daryl. "We all kind of ran it as a family. I think because it was our family, we all put a lot more into it. We are all competitive. We all did our best and we wanted to show each other. It really worked well.... No one was selfish. We all had egos, but we treated each other the same."

Lowell loved the fact that this was a family-owned company. Even for an entrepreneur with big ideas, working alongside family members seemed ideal.

The three Lohman brothers not only worked together, they played together. For many years, they participated on a flag football team. They were so passionate about the sport, and being teammates meant business actually came second during football season. But they didn't personally always need to be at the funeral homes or cemeteries because the businesses in essence "ran themselves," says Lowell, "because we had great managers."

On the football field, Lowell was, of course, the quarterback. He and his brothers were no longer boys separated by big age differences. Now, they were teammates among other grown men similar to them, in their twenties, thirties and forties, playing on flag football teams in various cities throughout Florida.

Lowell first played in Tallahassee when he was at FSU, then continued to play in leagues in Sarasota, Vero Beach, Palm Bay and Daytona Beach. (He was forty-three years old when he stopped playing.) He and his brothers, as well as his two sons, all had opportunities to play for winning teams, chasing championships.

Early on, when Lowell's boys, Brian and Ty, were too young to play on the flag football team, he took them to his games. As they got older, they played Little League Baseball and youth football. Lowell often coached them. Even in that role, he says he applied leadership skills similar to those he used in business. He refers to them as systems and structure. For example, he required the eleven- and twelve-year-old boys playing baseball to arrive at the field an hour before the game to take batting practice and play pepper, which is a repetitive routine where players are not far from a batter who continuously hits ground balls so hitting and fielding can be practiced. Lowell and Victor did that a lot when they were kids, even though Victor wasn't always willing. Lowell believed batting practice and playing pepper gave his young Little League players, and even the older ones at seventeen and eighteen years old in American Legion Baseball, a competitive advantage because most other teams weren't doing that.

Another "system" Lowell put into place when quarterbacking their men's flag football team was to write the plays on three-by-five laminated cards and keep those cards tucked in his shorts. In big games, while on the sideline when his team was on defense, he turned his back to the field and studied the cards in preparation for the next offensive series. To him, it was yet another system that gave him and his team a competitive advantage because he didn't see other quarterbacks doing that. It was also part of being a leader.

Lowell was the first flag football player to be voted the most valuable player in the national tournament twice. His team won the national championship one year, was runner-up another year, and ended up playing in the national tournament multiple times. In 1982, he was inducted into the U.S. Touch and Flag Football Hall of Fame, the first player from Florida to achieve that honor. He and Victor were also inducted into the Florida Flag Football League Hall of Fame for their individual contributions and together with their entire team.

On the football field and at the office, life for Lowell was good. But the same couldn't be said for his home life. He and Tina were limping along in their marriage, which had been strained for quite a long time. Divorce came seventeen years after their wedding. Brian and Ty continued to live with Tina, although a few years later, when Ty was fifteen years old, he came to live with Lowell.

During the 1980s when the Sloman Company continued adding funeral homes and cemeteries to their holdings, the partners grew more active in their industry's trade associations. Lowell served on the board of the Florida Cemetery Association and believed attending conventions was valuable because it helped the Lohmans keep up with the latest news and trends. But it also was educational with speakers presenting ideas and tips on marketing and sales, how to motivate one's self and employees, how to offer better training, and myriad other topics related to operating funeral homes and cemeteries. Lowell wrote pages and pages of notes – and twenty years later, he still has them. Many of the ideas, suggestions and practices he put into place. For example, at one meeting, several presenters talked about the Secrets of Closing Sales.

Excerpts from Lowell's Notes, 1970s – 1990s

If You Can't Close, You Can't Sell. To Close Is The Only Thing In Selling.

Closing Requires 1) Right Attitude; 2) Right Closing Key.

Closing Takes Courage: 1) Simple Rule – Try!

Be a Salesman – Not A Conversationalist.

Essentials Of Closing: 1) Confidence; 2) Desire To Close

A Planned Presentation Covers All Areas. Create A Want.

Be Persistent: Good Closers Try One More Time.

Closing Consciousness – Be Alert.

Close First In Your Own Mind!

Expect Success.

Know Every Objection!

Talk, Dress & Act Like Success.

Enthusiasm.

Sales Killers – 1) Overtalking; 2) Making Half A Presentation; 3) Too Much Pressure; 4) Negativism – Stay Away From Negative

People.

Buyer Becomes Abnormal At Time Of Buying: 1) Fear. You Must Reassure: A) Professional Attitude Reassures.

2) Fears: A) Lose Money; B) Goods Themselves; C) What Others May Think.

Adjust Tempo To Their Rate Of Thinking.

Decent Boldness – Wins Respect.

He Wants You To Step In & Make Up His Mind. Don't Talk After The Close.

Keys: 1) Make Every Call A Selling Call – A) Not A P.R. Man; 2) Keep Trying – Summarize, Close; 3) Beyond Any Doubt – Assumption – Don't Hesitate.... 6) Do Something – Takes Courage To Stop You.... Try For A Bigger Order.

Try! Persistence! Ask Why. Ask For A Decision Tonight; Ignore He Is Undecided; Needs Reassurance.

Refuse to Hear No.

Courage!

Don't Linger – Congratulate Him.

Be A Good Closer – Analyze Why.

Salesmanship – Art Of Pleasing People; I (is) Trouble (I vs. You or We).

Ego – Appeal to Prospect's.

Sell Yourself.

Attending conventions also provided opportunities for networking, which Lowell believes is imperative for anyone in business. "Get to know the main players, not only for acquisitions, but also when you may be ready to sell."

By 1989, the Sloman partners had become the second largest private owner of funeral homes and cemeteries in Florida. They owned twelve properties in Central and North Florida and employed about one hundred and fifty people. The company attracted attention.

The Slomans received a call from a representative of a large company in the industry offering to purchase their firms.

"I said I'm thirty-eight, thirty-nine years old, what do you mean?" Victor recalls. The representative flew in and Irv came up from Vero Beach. "We were sitting in there, and they threw a number at us," Victor says. "Then we said we'd meet with them tomorrow after we had a discussion about it at dinner that night. We went to dinner that night and I said let's throw another million on the price, and we all agreed. It was a great price. The thing that got our attention was that they were going to pay cash. We're not doing any payment plan. Now, we can either quit, or start again. I remember sitting with them the next day and throwing the extra million on top of their offer. They asked to excuse themselves and when they came back, they agreed to the price. That night we were sitting together as a family and we said, 'how much did we leave on the table? We should have asked for five million more.'"

> ## LOWELL'S INSIGHT
>
> **Money**
> Normally, you don't make a lot of money when you run a business. You make a lot of money when you sell it.

Today, Victor says the family should have sought other buyers rather than take the first and only offer.

Of the five partners, Daryl was the one who was reluctant to sell. "I wasn't thrilled with it because I was twenty-seven or twenty-eight years old. What am I going to do, play golf every day?"

Victor says he was only slightly hesitant to sell. "The

main reason for me was we would be disbanding our family as a business unit, which meant we wouldn't be talking every day. We were on the phone with Irv every week. So that part was hard. It was the end of the family business, and Irv was getting older. It turned out to be the right date and right time to sell."

Lowell agreed. Although he loved being in business with his family, he had visions of other entrepreneurial ventures, or at least dreams of building a company on his own.

The sale price: $13.5 million – an excellent payday because the Sloman Company didn't have a lot of debt.

Suddenly, Irv, Opal, Lowell, Victor and Daryl were millionaires.

What to do now?

Irv and Opal retired – again. Victor and Daryl agreed to continue in the jobs they were doing before the sale, although their roles expanded considerably with the company, Stillbrook, which purchased them. Victor stayed with Stillbrook, then Service Corporation International known as SCI, before deciding he would retire. He could go to the beach every day, and play golf. So that's what he did. Daryl was in charge of pre-need sales in Florida before Stillbrook was sold to SCI, the largest funeral and cemetery company in the world. Daryl continued with SCI for six to eight years before going to work for the next fifteen years selling final expense insurance for Senior Life Services. He was a Regional Sales Director.

For Lowell, the decision about what he would do after the sale was easy. "You're going to give me over a million dollars and I'm going to work for somebody? That doesn't compute in my brain."

So, the Lohman brother who doesn't mind taking risks, the entrepreneur who loves building companies, began seriously scouting for cemeteries and funeral homes he could buy. Even before the Sloman sale had closed, Lowell had started searching for properties. There was never a doubt in his mind that's what he would do. The only obstacle was where to buy. He was hamstrung slightly because a five-year non-compete clause meant he couldn't buy funeral homes and cemeteries in close proximity to those the Sloman Company had owned.

He found a cemetery for sale in Phoenix, Arizona.

Chapter 6

'Stop the World'

"In love, one and one are one."
Jean-Paul Sartre

Phoenix is twenty-one-hundred miles from Ormond Beach, but Lowell wasn't overly concerned about owning a cemetery that far away. He didn't need to be there on a daily basis. More importantly to him, Arizona was just like Florida in that it attracted large numbers of retirees and older people. The oldest baby boomers at the time were only forty-four, not yet old enough to be a primary target market, but they would be eventually.

Within thirty days of the Sloman sale, Lowell purchased Sun City Memorial Park in Phoenix. He also believed he would be able to buy a nearby funeral home, but that turned out not to be the case. Still, Lowell was once again in business for himself, by himself. He called his company Lohman Enterprises. True to his nature, he wasted no time looking for more properties. The first one he found, and purchased, was Beaches Memorial Park Cemetery in Atlantic Beach, Florida, which is next door to Jacksonville Beach. Less than a two-hour drive from Ormond Beach, it was just outside the area where he was prohibited from owning a cemetery or funeral home because of the non-compete clause in the Sloman sale.

Owning two cemeteries was good, but Lowell wasn't in business to operate a small company. More cemeteries would be better. So, he continued to search. A friend told him about one for sale in Marietta, Georgia, a suburb of Atlanta. It was Cheatham Hill Memorial Park. Lowell inquired about it. Soon he was on his way to negotiate and finalize the purchase. Filled with optimism and high expectations, his arrival in Atlanta set him on a path to the kind of life-changing event usually found in storybooks with idyllic endings. This was the storybook's beginning.

August 24, 1990, Lowell says, was the day that changed his life.

Following a business meeting, he asked where he might find "a nice, classy place with classy ladies." He was told to go to Otto's, an upscale piano lounge in the Buckhead section of Atlanta where the musicians often play the kind of music with lyrics Frank Sinatra would sing, like "New York, New York" or "Strangers in the Night." Sitting by himself at the bar, Lowell watched for about thirty minutes as a half-dozen men and women were gathered nearby and appeared to be having a great time. He was particularly mesmerized by one of the women. "I remember my brain saying, 'only in Atlanta do you find a lady like this.' I said to myself, 'That is the most vivacious, gorgeous, fun female I have ever seen.'" And he hadn't even met her.

She noticed him, but almost in passing. "Honestly, I just wasn't thinking, 'Who is this guy that I need to leave my date to talk with?' I just thought he was like the rest of our group, that he was a fun-loving person out on a Friday night."

Eventually, she and the others invited Lowell, along with a woman also sitting at the bar, to join the group as they drank a round of tequila together. Not just shots, but body shots, something Lowell had never done or seen. Lick your partner's neck, add some salt, place a slice of lime in his or her mouth, then lick the neck, drink the shot and kiss the lime out of their mouth. Lowell participated, just not with the blonde who so captivated him. She was there with her boyfriend. Soon, the fun ended and everyone departed. Lowell only knew the woman's name was Nancy – and that she had a boyfriend. He didn't know anything else about her.

The next night, Lowell went back to Otto's, hoping he might see Nancy there. Instead, he saw only her boyfriend, Casey, and the two of them talked for a while. Lowell recalls the boyfriend was only interested in talking about himself while Lowell only wanted to talk about Nancy. When he learned Nancy was attending a wedding without her boyfriend, Lowell thought that showed they probably weren't a serious couple. But what really made an impression was when Nancy's boyfriend said she was the 1981 homecoming queen at Ohio State University.

"As soon as he said that, my logical brain said, 'stop the world', Lowell says. "It changed my life one-hundred percent." The reason, he says, is he knew how difficult it was to be chosen homecoming queen at a massive school like OSU, and it wasn't just about beauty. It was about being a good student, a good person with strong core values, and an OSU Buckeye who could be an outstanding representative for the university. Lowell had dated a homecoming queen in high school and also a member of the homecoming queen's court. So, he was more impressed than ever with Nancy having been the homecoming queen at OSU. But he was also a bit perplexed: She was thirty years old, had never been married, and she was apparently very successful. "What is she doing out here?" Lowell remembers thinking.

Casey said they were meeting at a restaurant across the

street after the wedding Nancy was attending. Ten minutes after he left, Lowell followed. He went to the same place. "I walked in and thought she's the most gorgeous woman I've ever seen. We talked awhile. I tried to get her to go back to Otto's. Bottom line answer is they left."

The next day, Lowell finalized the purchase of the cemetery. He had brought in two of his managers from Florida to help with the transition of the business. Lowell told them about the "pretty blonde named Nancy" he had met. For the next several days, in the evenings, they all went to Otto's hoping Nancy would be there. But it was when they were crossing busy Peachtree Road five nights after they had first met that one of them asked Lowell if he noticed the blonde crossing the street in the opposite direction, and that she seemed to be looking at him. Lowell was concerned about getting across the street in the traffic, but then he saw her. "Nancy," he yelled.

"I couldn't believe it. She turned around."

"Hi Lowell," she said.

"You can't make this stuff up," says Lowell as he tells the story twenty-seven years later.

Lowell's group, Nancy and her friend, Mary Frey, all went to Otto's. But long before Lowell wanted the night to end, Nancy and Mary had to go.

"You cannot leave. I've been searching for you for three days," he told her. "I'll beg – and I do not beg. Just stay ten more minutes."

But before she left, she did give him her business card. Nancy Shively (she had legally changed the spelling from Schaible) worked for Eastman Kodak, selling copiers and copy products to government agencies. Eastman Kodak took its business cards seriously because the employee's photo was on the card. It was the kind of personalized touch that reinforced the importance of images for this photography and copier company. The cards weren't designed to be given out to just anyone. But that didn't matter to Lowell. "Please don't do that card thing," he told her. As she started to leave, he began telling her that she was his Cinderella and that he couldn't live without her.

"I thought he was charming, but didn't think I should stay alone with people whom I'd just met," Nancy recalls.

Nancy and Mary left. Lowell's heart sank.

"When they left, my brain said 'Strangers in the Night. There probably wasn't anything there.' People have asked me would I have called her, and my answer was I probably would have, but I don't know. I didn't get tons of feedback from her."

Outside, Mary told Nancy she had been too aloof – and that she should go back and have a cocktail with Lowell.

"I reapplied my lipstick, fluffed my hair and went back inside," says Nancy. "He had such a wonderful smile on when I came back in. I will never forget that. He was just so glad I was back. That's what his expression said."

Most conversations between two people who are just getting to know each other eventually reach the point where each person discusses his or her work. Of course, most people aren't in the type of business that was Lowell's. "He told me he owned cemeteries and funeral homes – and I thought, nobody would say that to impress a girl," Nancy says. "Honestly, even though I had had a father and brother who died, as well as grandparents who had died, I never contemplated who owned the cemeteries. I just assumed they were owned by a municipality. I had no idea someone could privately own them."

Nancy was curious about his business. And she really

wanted to know more about this man. They made a lunch date for the next day at a revolving restaurant overlooking Atlanta.

"It was through that lunch that I realized this was a really good person," she says. "He's a fun guy, charismatic, and I'm attracted to him. I thought I need to go see his cemetery, not to prove that he really owned it. It wasn't anything like that. But I wanted to get a sense of what he was so passionate about, what was so important to him, and to take a look at a cemetery in a different light, from the perspective that someone is responsible for the well-being of the cemetery."

Lowell was smitten. "Casey was in a lot of trouble; he just didn't know it yet," says Lowell, who returned to Ormond Beach, but was scheduled to be back in Atlanta for business two weeks later. He was back in three days. After several dates over the next few days, both Lowell and Nancy had the same thought: this felt right.

Nancy went to see Lowell's business – Cheatham Hill Memorial Park, the cemetery he just purchased.

"You couldn't have scripted a better cemetery for someone to go see if you want to know what it meant to be in the cemetery business. It is truly one of the most beautiful cemeteries I have ever seen. Still is, to this day," she says. (It is now owned by the Lohmans' good friend, Christine Hunsaker and Hunsaker Partners). "A lot of cemeteries don't have good roads because they're very expensive to pave, maintain and repair. This cemetery had beautiful streets, beautiful curbs and beautiful paved sidewalks that weaved through the gardens of the cemetery. It has beautiful rolling hills and a beautiful entrance. When I arrived, I saw a woman sitting on a hill with her little girl. I'm thinking she's telling her about that woman's mother, her grandmother. That's exactly what a cemetery is about. It's this whole idea that we have a place to reflect, remember and tell stories. It's this link to the past. It's this connection for people. It all just came together for me. I understood why cemeteries are so important. It made me realize what a beautiful business Lowell is in. I didn't know the business side of it at the time. I just understood what it meant to the community, what it meant to people."

Lowell invited Nancy to go with him to Phoenix. But he wasn't thinking about business, although he could check on his business, the cemetery, while he was there. His interest was in wooing Nancy and impressing her. He thought a trip to Phoenix and nearby Sedona seemed like the perfect getaway to spend time together.

Immediately after that trip, Lowell returned to Ormond Beach, knowing he and Nancy were meant to be together. Lowell, however, had to first end another relationship that had evolved into an engagement.

"I sit down with my fiancée and tell her it's not working. I wrote her a big check. We'd been together a couple of years, and she deserved it. I was lucky enough to have the ability to do it. It was the right thing to do with her. It wasn't complicated. My brother, Victor, says if he ever dies and comes back, he wants to come back as my girlfriend. I flew back to Atlanta. My son, Ty, tells this story: 'My dad left and didn't come back for three months.' I pretty well didn't."

Nancy wasn't engaged to her boyfriend. She had previously decided that relationship wasn't progressing, and she didn't see a future for it. Some years earlier, she had been engaged twice. But neither of those felt right. So, she moved on. It was not, she says, that she was afraid of commitment or marriage. She just hadn't met the right person. She remembers thinking, "I'm definitely not going to compromise. I'm not going to settle for a life that's going to have any type of regrets in it. I don't want to walk on eggshells. I don't want to be held back. If I don't feel completely lifted up in life by someone, I was not getting married. I thought maybe they weren't out there.... I pretty much thought I was meant to be single."

She also wasn't focused on the idea of getting married and having children. "I always knew that I would have children if I met the right person, and they wanted to have children. But I always knew I was very career-oriented, that I liked making money and carrying my own weight, that I was very independent. So, the idea of being a stay-at-home mom and not have monetary freedom never appealed to me. I wanted independence and I wanted financial freedom.... If I met someone who really wanted to have children, and it was a great partnership, and financially we could do it together, we would. However, if all of that wasn't there, I knew it wasn't going to happen."

Lowell already had two sons – and he had no interest in having more children. Plus, he was forty-five when he met Nancy, who was thirty. The age difference was bit of a concern to Lowell. Not really for himself, but he thought Nancy might think they were too many years apart. Lowell also thought, if they got together, she might decide she really wants children. The courtship turned very quickly to a committed relationship, but there was no talk about a possible marriage. Within a month or two from the day they met, Lowell moved in with Nancy in her house in Atlanta.

She had chosen this Southern metropolitan city three years earlier after she was first hired by Eastman Kodak in Rochester, New York where she was living and working at the time as an assistant director of sales for a Marriott Hotel. Like Lowell, her career in sales didn't start until after she graduated from college, although she once had a part-time job in retail when she was in high school. But she didn't study sales or business in college. She majored in floraculture, then discovered it didn't fit her skills or talent or interest. So, she switched majors and earned her degree in human ecology, the study of human behavior, a sort of mix of psychology and sociology. That, however, wasn't a field that easily translated to a job for a new college graduate. Having been fiercely independent as a child and for most of her young life, Nancy felt she had good coping skills and resiliency even though she wasn't entirely filled with self-confidence. So, although she had no hospitality experience, she was hired as the sales director for a catering firm and felt she could succeed.

"They could tell I probably had this innate ability to sell. They could also see that I was a hard worker. I've always been able to sell and I've been able to sell myself. I think that ability to have a positive conversation with people comes naturally."

When Nancy and Lowell met, she was on her way to becoming Eastman Kodak's Regional Sales Director for Government Markets, assisting with the marketing efforts across all product lines in the Southeastern United States. Her marketing and sales experience was immediately helpful to Lowell, although not in an official position.

Chapter 7

Sales Managers, 'Try Saying Thank You'

"The ultimate test of management is performance."
Peter F. Drucker

The pre-need sales counselors at Lowell's cemeteries used a presentation kit, a book with pages highlighting features and benefits for customers. Nancy quickly noticed room for improvements because the pages were copies of copies of copies – and mostly black ink on green paper.

> LOWELL'S INSIGHT
>
> **Employee Training**
> In the cemetery and funeral business, and then in the apartment business, we created video training tapes. On the first day, new employees listened and watched those tapes. That guaranteed that every new employee was initially trained by the best people in the company. Assuming that every manager in the company is a great trainer is a bad assumption.

"They were terrible. Here I am in copy products with these amazing electronic printers that are as long as a room. So, I took all of the kit pages and I worked with one of my friends at

Kodak and we re-designed every single one of his pages.... Same content, but better text, graphics and photos, all in full color," she says. "I think a big part of a person's success is having the tools to do the job well. I think every single part of your business is a reflection on your professionalism."

LOWELL'S INSIGHT

Training Manuals

It's important to have detailed training manuals for all personnel. Ours included chapters on hiring, training, meetings, leads, leadership, incentive programs and contests, family services, telemarketing and referrals.

She also helped Lowell record and duplicate VHS training tapes used by his sales managers and sales counselors. Additionally, at Cheatham Hill Memorial Park, she incorporated into the offices Civil War paintings, posters and artifacts. The cemetery is adjacent to historic Cheatham Hill National Battlefield and Kennesaw Mountain National Battlefield Park.

Lowell continued to search for more cemeteries to buy, especially in his new hometown, the metropolitan Atlanta area. Over time, he purchased one in Lithonia, another in Dunwoody, and another in Cherokee County. "You can't think of a better business market to be in than the Atlanta market. It wasn't easy to find them there because the good ones weren't for sale," he says.

Curb appeal, the overall appearance, and of course, the number of burials per month and per year were primary factors Lowell considered when looking to buy. For all of his properties, including those in other cities, he was always supremely confident before he purchased them that he could increase sales.

"Most of the cemeteries had tremendous potential, but you often had an owner that was kind of sitting there waiting for someone to die." Lowell wasn't going to wait on business. "No, sir. I rolled in with a (pre-need) sales force. I brought an experienced manager in. We trained our new team. We did everything else. I guarantee you that within the first year, I almost doubled what they did the (previous) year in sales at every cemetery I bought."

Of course, true to his philosophy in owning a business, Lowell didn't get involved in the day-to-day operations. He tried to hire great managers who understood they were in the people business – and let them manage the business. Lowell took the advice he gives to other entrepreneurs: Work on the business, not in the business.

LOWELL'S INSIGHT

Be the Cheerleader

As a business owner, ninety percent of what I do every day is be our cheerleader. Every time I go to the office, we address things and get it done. If I address someone pretty hard, if I have to point out something they're not doing or not doing well, or discipline them, I go back and rescue them before I leave. I always search for something positive to tell them. I think that's part of being the cheerleader.

"I'm very good at delegating. I think I have good 'feel', and that's a big word in any business. There's tons of smart people, but if you don't have 'feel', and understand what others around you need, I don't think you can grow as quick or fast as you could have. The one thing that I found is I am not detail-oriented, but I am incredibly structured."

Among other things, that structure meant having

systems, monitoring, and having training methods and manuals for sales managers and salespeople. One of his manuals entitled Sales Management Guidelines included sections on Sales Management, Hiring/Training, Meetings, Contests, Family Service, Telemarketing and Referrals. In one part of the Sales Management section is a page listing the reasons managers fail. The reasons could apply to almost any type of business.

Excerpt as Written in the 1990s
SALES MANAGEMENT GUIDELINES
WHY MANAGERS FAIL

1. They reach a comfort zone.
2. They are insecure. This is caused by inexperience, or not knowing all phases of training and management.
3. They have the salesman's point of view, not the Company's.
4. They try to please everybody.
5. They fail to set an example.
6. You are in the center of the stage. If you do not set an example, they lose faith in the (leader).
7. There are three ways to teach: by example, by example, by example.

Additional Excerpts
LEADERSHIP
- A top manager must be interested in people
- A top manager loses many close friendships
- Keep a firm hand on meetings – discourage arguments
- A business is not a democracy
- What is the role of a sales manager?
- Respect, not like, is important

- Do not let a Counselor back you down

HIRING
- The hiring of a salesman is more important than the training of the salesman
- Salesmen are born, not made
- 4 ways – Newspapers, word of mouth, piracy & Personnel agencies
- Run ads on Sunday and Monday
- Monday and Tuesday are hiring days
- Hire well ahead – many bad salesmen are hired because the manager is caught behind the Eight Ball
- Do not hire close friends or relatives
- Negative traits when hiring:
  1. Bad mouths his old boss
  2. Had been his own boss
  3. Domestic problems
- Don't hire the best of a bad bunch
- Anticipate salespeople leaving

As the owner, Lowell did not adhere to his own advice to not hire "close friends or relatives." His youngest son, Ty, worked in pre-need sales several summers. And Victor's son, Christopher, also came to Atlanta and spent time working in pre-need sales at Lowell's cemeteries. For Lowell, having family members working in the business was ideal.

In one of the training manuals, there was a section about the importance of sales managers being supportive and showing appreciation to their salespeople. The origin of the content is unknown, but the training manual included a compilation of articles, notes and information from various sources. The guidelines for sales managers could apply to managers in most businesses.

Excerpt as Written in the 1990s
SALES MANAGEMENT GUIDELINES

TRY SAYING THANK YOU

People work for love and money. Few of us ever seem to get enough of either. There are not great behavioral science secrets to good management. If you will give top priority to supporting and paying your people you will be blessed with results beyond your dreams.

Managers often think of themselves as systems specialist or problems solvers or function experts. They lose sight of the common sense practicality of getting others committed to doing things for them willingly. The essence of good management (is) letting people know what you expect, inspecting what is done, and supporting those things that are done well.

We don't even know the design limitations of a human being. All we do know is that even the most committed people seldom exceed 15% or 20% of their brain capacity in a normal day's work.

Average people can easily double or triple their output without even exerting themselves. If managers would begin thinking in terms of doing things for their people, instead of to them, we would see productivity increases off the scales.

Make a list of everyone who works for you. Before the week is out tell each one personally what he has contributed this week and how much you appreciate his efforts.

Set up informal visits with your people. Listen and use your eyes to pick up on what is going on. Don't look for problems, look for strengths and things done well. Make something out of every positive thing you can find. As a manager, your words and actions carry impact much greater than you expect. Just a small effort with these techniques will have almost immediate effect. A concentrated, disciplined, and sustained thrust in these directors will produce incredible returns.

Publish everything positive you can find. Print is cheap. Its rewards are long-lasting.

Put positive notes on everything and send them back to everyone.

How innovative can you be? Do you realize the impact you have on others? Can you reduce or eliminate the negatives in your dealings with your people? Will you do the searching and analysis necessary to uncover positive contributions? Can you name the strengths of all of your people? Can you say something complimentary to everyone by the end of the week?

As simple and as straightforward as all this is, it is really a tremendously difficult professional challenge. Just how good are you as a professional manager? If results are produced by committed people, just how much love and money can you spread around to build that commitment and those results? Go, do something nice for someone. Do it today!

Personally, it didn't take Lowell and Nancy much time before they realized their relationship was "perfect," as Nancy says, and they "got very serious, very quickly." So, they bought a house together in Marietta, a suburb of Atlanta.

> ## LOWELL'S INSIGHT
>
> **Financial Statements**
>
> When I got into business many years ago, I didn't understand financial statements. I read three or four books on how you analyze financial statements. That's important. I think half the owners of businesses out there really don't understand what a financial statement accomplishes.

"It's one of the things that I think made me realize that Lowell was such a giving and trusting person. We knew pretty much right away that we could trust each other. He put the down payment on the house, but he put it in both of our names. Before we ever talked about marriage, he did that."

With Lowell having two houses in Ormond Beach, and Nancy owning her house and condo in the Atlanta area, the couple set about selling all four after they bought their house together.

Both Lowell and Nancy were happy with their relationship, but they didn't talk about getting married. "It never came up because I was not going to mention it," says Nancy. "I knew I probably didn't have to. I didn't need to pressure him. Things were going really well." After they had been together for a little more than a year, the idea of marriage came up in an unexpected way.

Nancy invited Lowell to go with her on a business trip to Washington, D.C. They could stay for a few days after the business meetings and it would be a fun getaway for the two of them. Lowell loved the idea, and then he said, "When we go up there, why don't we get married?" Just like that, the idea of marriage was suddenly out there. And what did Nancy think? "I loved it. I booked a non-refundable airline ticket for him. That's what I always say jokingly. Of course, I was thrilled. I guess I sort of sensed it would progress to that. So, I never felt like I needed to give him an ultimatum."

LOWELL'S INSIGHT

Read Books
Reading is important. People in business should read. Years ago, I used to read a lot on marketing and sales. I attack books on leadership and the stock market. A lot of people say they don't have the time to read. It's all about attitude. You can find time to read a book if you really want to. Business owners who say they don't have the time to read are doing the urgent things, not the important.

Nancy's friend, Valerie Hughes in Hay Market, Virginia arranged for the couple to stay at the historic Bailiwick Inn, a bed and breakfast in Fairfax, Virginia, and she arranged for a justice of the peace to come to the courtyard and officiate the wedding. "We had a beautiful little ceremony," Nancy says. It was October 10, 1991, a little more than thirteen months after the couple met August 26, 1990.

Life was good and business was good. Lowell saw no reason to travel for business. Phoenix wasn't that far from Atlanta by plane, but when he could concentrate his efforts in Atlanta, why own a cemetery in Phoenix? So, he called his friend, Stan Stobierski, who owned the neighboring funeral home and offered to sell the property to him. "I said, 'I'll make you a great deal. Give me just enough down so we have a deal, then pay me the balance over five years.' Then I threw out a figure that I thought would make sense for both of us. It was a win-win deal and he jumped on it."

The sale was for $400,000.

In the early to mid-90s, SCI and Stewart Enterprises were two of the nation's largest companies that owned cemeteries and funeral homes. They were actively bidding on properties in Atlanta. Lowell, of course, knew executives from both companies because one of his Lowellisms is for business owners to get to know the main players in their industry. That works to their advantage when it comes time to sell. Lowell also was known because he was active in both the Georgia Cemetery Association and Florida Cemetery Association. By this time, he had served on both associations' board of directors.

Lowell saw what was happening in his industry in the booming Atlanta area – and he decided there was an opportunity to sell his four cemeteries. Owning four in one metropolitan area gave him leverage. Clustering businesses in one area rather than trying to be in too many geographical areas was another bit of business wisdom that Lowell had learned from his experiences with the Sloman company, which owned funeral homes and cemeteries scattered in various locales in Central and East Central Florida. And, of course, Lowell had owned the cemetery in Phoenix. He still owned one in Atlantic Beach – and he had bought and begun renovating a building for a funeral home in Jacksonville Beach about eight miles from the cemetery. But having four properties in the Atlanta area was significant and valuable.

"Anytime you can cluster your companies in a smaller geographical area, you will run them more efficiently and make more money," he says. It's still difficult to control multiple locations with extensive travel among the managers and staff. And, as growth occurs, so does the benefit of economies of scale.

One of his Lowellisms in business pertains to timing, knowing when to act. "Every business has a moment. Economy, interest rates, market changes, competition, etc. Don't wait too long if the time is right."

Lowell realized this was one of those moments for his company.

Rick Baldwin, a close friend who had owned funeral homes in the Orlando, Florida area and now worked for Stewart Enterprises, encouraged Lowell to sell to Stewart if he was ready. A deal was negotiated, and Stewart purchased Lowell's four Atlanta area cemeteries for $4.3 million.

After the sale, he no longer owned any businesses in Atlanta. Rick convinced Lowell to become vice president for Stewart Enterprise's Southeast Division's Atlanta area. Of course, Lowell was already settled in the city, primarily because being with Nancy was like a dream come true. He missed his family in Florida and missed living in Ormond Beach, but he didn't ever suggest to Nancy that they leave Atlanta.

"I think because he knew how much I loved Atlanta, he was willing to love it with me. He was maybe willing to let Florida go," she says. But knowing how much he yearned for Florida, and seeing him traveling from Atlanta to Jacksonville Beach and Atlantic Beach to attend to his businesses, she thought, "I could help with this.... I told him if a position opened up in Florida, then I think I should take it. He never pushed me to quit my job or leave my career. I think that was really admirable that Lowell never said this is what we're going to do. He never pushed that down my throat. It just shows how good he is in business strategy. He just let that be my idea."

The couple looked at houses in Ponte Vedra Beach, Florida, next door to Jacksonville Beach. For Nancy, she wanted any move to be the only move they would make – forever, whether they bought a house or built a house. She grew up the daughter of a father whose career was in the military, and although the family didn't move as much as some, it was enough, especially when she counted the moves during her adult life. She was born in Lincoln, Nebraska, but when she was a young child, the family – mother, father, sisters and brother moved to Sacramento, California. And, then when she was nine years old, they moved to Columbus, Ohio, where she lived until after graduating from college. She worked for Hyatt Hotels in Columbus until she was promoted to the Hyatt in Lexington, Kentucky. Then she continued her hotel sales career in Rochester, New York before she was hired by Kodak and relocated to Atlanta. She loved Atlanta, and felt she could easily stay there forever. In fact, she always thought she would. She asked Lowell if he would promise they would stay in Ponte Vedra Beach if they moved there. He just couldn't make that promise, he told her. "If we moved to Ormond Beach, could we live there forever?" she asked him. "'Oh, yes,'" he replied, "'I'll build your dream home!'"

On the weekend of July 4, 1994, nearly four years after they met, the couple moved to Ormond Beach, renting a furnished condo in a high-rise building on the beachside while scouting out locations to build a home. Of course, Lowell was excited to be back where he had spent so many years with his son, Ty, and with his brother, Victor. This was home to Lowell. He knew a lot of people and a lot of people knew Lowell Lohman.

The couple bought riverfront property on John Anderson Drive from homebuilder friends of Lowell's, the Strassers, and began working with them and an architect to build a home.

Eastman Kodak had moved the Lohmans to Florida and had placed Nancy in charge of a territory surrounding Ormond Beach, from Orlando to Jacksonville. It was a good job, but a little off the path up the corporate ladder she was following in Atlanta. It was really more of a lateral move for Nancy. Even so, she still loved working for Eastman Kodak. She managed a team of eight salespeople and a budget with annual revenues of more than $8 million. Her expertise and high profile also led to her being a guest speaker to various groups such as the American Marketing Association's Central Florida Chapter in Orlando where she spoke on Personal Selling – Kodak Style. The group's advance publicity about Nancy's presentation noted it would focus on "those sales techniques we can apply to our everyday marketing and community efforts. The extremely competitive nature of her industry gives Ms. Lohman deep insight into the different aspects of personal selling...."

At Beaches Memorial Park Cemetery in Atlantic Beach and the Beaches Funeral Home in Jacksonville Beach – Lowell brought both of his sons into his businesses. But he says they were too young and not ready. So, that didn't work out. Lowell later sold the funeral home and cemetery for $3 million. Ty stayed on and continued working pre-need sales before leaving to work in sales at an Internet company in Jacksonville.

Once again, Lowell, the entrepreneur and business-builder, was out of business. He owned no funeral homes or cemeteries, and no other businesses.

Nancy suggested he take some time to relax rather than rushing back into business, whatever that might be. Lowell did just that – for a little while. He played golf, but his concentration was not on the game. Racing in his mind were thoughts of business, what he might do, what he didn't want to do. Certainly, doing nothing was not an option for an experienced businessman who knew success, had made it happen, had lived it. Idleness and contentment, at least when they pertain to business, aren't even in Lowell's dictionary.

For the past seven years or so as he was buying and selling cemeteries and the funeral home, Lowell realized he still loved the business. But he felt something missing: it wasn't a family business. It just wasn't as much fun being the only one who got excited when he bought and sold properties, and was building his company. Those thoughts were the genesis of another Lowellism: "To buy makes you happy. To share makes you happier!"

Chapter 8

Think of the Possibilities

"What the mind can conceive and believe,
the mind can achieve."
Napoleon Hill

Lowell had an idea. It may have been his best idea *ever* – in more ways than one. Oh, the possibilities, the potential, the enormity of it all, he really had no doubt. It wasn't an idea born in an ah-ha moment. More of a natural coming together of beginnings and endings in the ebb and flow of life – and business. So, on this day in 1996, with grand visions, and completely head-over-heels in love with his wife, Lowell explained the idea to her – using words phrased in a manner every salesperson knows.

"Nancy, if you will go back to school and get your funeral director's license, I will build the nicest funeral home you have ever seen. I'll build it, but you're going to run it."

Nancy's reaction: surprise and shock.

She had never worked in the funeral business. Never thought about working in the funeral business. Plus, she already had a successful marketing career.

For a few moments, she thought about Lowell's idea. And then, she responded, with her warm personality and caring manner on full display. "I can't be a funeral director. I wear fuchsia."

Although Lowell didn't fully appreciate the humor in her response, it was the kind of disarming comment that he knew was one of the reasons Nancy would be the perfect person in the business. And, of course, he already had his storybook romance, always telling his single friends they could stop looking for Cinderella because he married her. So, it was hard for him to imagine anything better than the two of them working together. It reminded Lowell of advice he received many years earlier from his stepfather, Irv Silverman, who said there are two important things in the world: "The most important is the person you choose to spend the rest of your life with. The second most important is the career you choose that lets the two of you enjoy your life together. Whatever is third is so far behind the first two, it doesn't matter."

Once, early in their relationship, Lowell and Nancy contemplated how they might someday merge the professional and personal sides of their lives. But this was just talk, just dreaming. And, at the time, Lowell said he needed a wife more than he needed a business partner. So, Nancy didn't give any more thought to the two of them being in business together. But that was then. This was now.

To Lowell, it was clear as a sunny day that Nancy would be the ideal business partner and funeral director. She's a savvy businesswoman and excellent saleswoman. Her outgoing personality and temperament, matched with compassion, sincerity, and genuineness in her caring seemed to be the very definition of a person who should be helping grieving individuals and families during one of the most difficult times of their lives.

But become a funeral director?

Her immediate light-hearted response that she couldn't

be a funeral director because she wore fuchsia bought her a moment of time, a pause to understand what all this might mean. She really had never considered this as the kind of work she would do. Of course, being with Lowell for the past six years, she had seen the cemetery business up close. But that was still from the outside looking in, and certainly not the same as being a part of it. Plus, the cemetery business wasn't the same as the funeral home business.

Her first thought, though, after overcoming her initial surprise, was not whether she was interested in this type of work, or even suited for it. The question she asked herself: would people be able to tell how much she cared? That, she says, was really important to her.

"I know I care and I have a big heart. I know I feel badly when people are hurting, but I'd never been tested like that. I'd never had to make sure people knew that. I mean, I think my friends and family see and sense that, but I'd never chosen a career that requires that. That's the first thing I thought – will people see in my heart how much I care? That's going to be really important. I never had to contemplate that before. I don't think a lot of people contemplate that. I was worried about that, at first, because I socialize, I can be loud and animated, I make jokes.... Will I need to change my demeanor in public? Will I need to change the way I dress? How will people feel when they run into me because now I'm a funeral director? I'm not just Nancy Lohman. Because I had commuted to Orlando and Jacksonville the entire time I had lived in Florida and worked for Kodak, I was gone most of the time from our community. A lot of people knew me, and I had made a lot of friends here easily because I was a Lohman. But I hadn't invested a lot of time in the community because I didn't have the chance to. I was always working."

Not traveling so much for work would certainly be a plus. But deep down, she had to ask herself if she really wanted to be a funeral director. For many, it's a calling, a desire to care for families during their grief, to help people of all ages navigate everything that comes with losing a loved one. For others, it's a desire to work in the back of the funeral home, taking care of the bodies, embalming and preparing them for the funeral, the science of the funeral director's job rather than being with families making arrangements and coordinating the funeral services.

At the time, becoming a licensed funeral director in Florida required one to attend mortuary science school for at least a year – more if the person didn't already have a college degree. And all students who preferred a dual license so they could legally manage a funeral home had to not only learn embalming, they had to embalm a minimum of ten bodies, even if they had no plans to work that side of the business. Then, after completing school, there was a one-year internship, working under the tutelage of a licensed funeral director.

Nancy really did think Lowell's idea had merit. She believed completely in him as a businessman, as an entrepreneur. She could give up her frequent business travel, and because she already had a college degree, it would take only a year in school. And, she knew Lowell's passion for business, especially when he was working with family, would help her succeed.

It took her a few weeks to get her arms around the idea – and to come up with a plan. She visited St. Petersburg (FL) Junior College which offered a mortuary science program. She then secured permission from her boss, John Braun, to work part time.

In May, 1997, immediately after a groundbreaking ceremony to build Ormond Funeral Home in Ormond Beach, Nancy began one year of classes to become a licensed funeral director. Even while in school and still working, she helped Lowell with ideas and plans for what they wanted this new funeral home to look like. They visited numerous funeral homes and talked with many funeral directors and others in the industry. Of course, Lowell, with his years of experience, already had some definite ideas. And, he was willing to tap his deep pockets to make this a grand and luxurious funeral home for their Ormond Beach community and for Nancy to run. He was not only ready to get back in the business, he was giddy about the possibilities. He truly believed this was the right time, the right place, and the right person. This vision, this idea, this plan.

Lowell with his maternal Grandfather,
Jesse Holland, about 1947.

Lowell, left, and his brother, Victor, in front of the
family's home on Bonita Avenue in
Vero Beach, Florida.

Lowell with his Vero Beach High School football and baseball coach, Coach Ken Barrett, in 1962.

The quarterback in his senior year in high school in 1962.

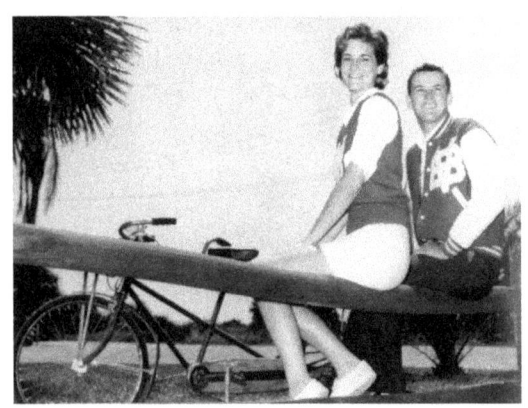

At Vero Beach High School, Lowell and
Stevie Guerin were voted
Most Athletic in 1963.

Lowell was named Captain and Most
Valuable Player on his college baseball team.

Brothers, left to right, Lowell, Victor and Daryl playing flag football in 1982.

In Flag Football, Lowell was the quarterback.

"Jump on these shoulders and hang on."

Lowell celebrating with teammates after winning the National Championship in Flag Football in 1981.

Florida Flag Football Hall of Fame Trophies for the Lohman brothers. Left to right, Lowell's son, Ty; Lowell; Victor; and Victor's son, Christopher, in 2009.

Florida Flag Football League Hall of Fame Ceremony in 2011.

Edgar Lohman, Lowell's father, in the 1980s.

Lowell's mother, Opal, and Lowell's stepfather, Irv Silverman, in the 1970s.

The Lohman Family at Chateau Lake Louise, Banff, Canada, 2016.

The Lohman-Odom-Holland Families' annual gathering at Christmas in 2004.

Nancy Lohman's family in Ohio in 2009. In the back row, left to right, Darrin Smith and Lowell Lohman; second row, left to right, Carolyn Smith, Ashley Johnson, Chase Koenigs (baby), Matt Koenigs, Nancy Lohman, Andrew Ries and Richard Schaffter; first row, left to right, Hallie Smith, Leanne Koenigs, Ann Weiss and Marilyn Schaffter.

Chapter 9

'You Have to Make Things Happen'

"It requires a better type of mind to seek out and to support
or to create the new than to follow the worn paths of success."
John D. Rockefeller

On August 30, 1998, sixty-one years after the death of John D. Rockefeller – once the world's richest man – remembrances and memorabilia of the controversial businessman and philanthropist were on display to hundreds of people who gathered to mark the opening of a grand, new building – Ormond Funeral Home – situated less than three miles west of where he died at his winter home known as The Casements, on the eastern bank of the Halifax River. The oil tycoon was, of course, both revered and reviled in his lifetime, but in Ormond Beach, where many knew him as Neighbor John, he was mostly loved. And after all these years, he was still remembered as the city's most famous resident. He died at the age of ninety-seven on May 23, 1937, just twenty-six months shy of his frequently professed goal of living one-hundred years.

Rockefeller's life and extraordinary business success may have been different from others in Ormond Beach, but he was just like most people when it came to the topic of death. He simply didn't discuss it. "Never did he speak of death in

109

relation to himself; rather did he speak always of life, of activity, of accomplishment," according to his son. In that regard, Rockefeller surely would have admired this stately, new funeral home and the business vision it signified for Lowell and Nancy.

If Lowell's business plan and ideas were correct, this new facility was unlike any other funeral home, and would serve as the foundation and blueprint for growth, adding more funeral homes and cemeteries while also bringing in more family members to be part of the business.

"Most people wait for things to happen. Sometimes you have to make things happen!" says Lowell, reciting one of his Lowellisms.

With symbolism befitting a museum, including artifacts such as a displayed, enclosed genuine casements window from Rockefeller's home, artists' paintings of local historic sites, and a six-foot by six-foot model display of the one-hundred-and-five-year-old Ormond Hotel, which had been demolished six years earlier in 1992, visitors on this day could easily feel they had stepped inside a museum or perhaps the lobby of a fancy, high-end hotel.

Adjacent to the reception area was the aptly named Rockefeller Chapel, which would seat one-hundred-and-sixty people. Down one hall was the Casement's room, a private area for families who would be attending funeral services. Both Lowell and Nancy loved the idea of incorporating Ormond Beach's history and heritage. Nancy believed it added a welcoming feel to a hometown funeral home. A story in a funeral industry magazine shortly after the grand opening drew the same conclusion: "To say that the Ormond community is impressed by this 'museum' concept of a funeral home is an understatement. To quote a somewhat overenthusiastic visitor:

'It almost makes the thought of dying easier.'"

Most of the approximately seven-hundred local and area residents in attendance probably didn't feel that way, but they were at least curious enough and interested enough to see this new place they had watched being built during the past sixteen months. The immediate reaction from many, Lowell remembers, was "one word, 'Wow'. You're not expecting it. You have in your mind a vision of funeral homes. This one's different."

For many in Ormond Beach, this day was a special occasion not only because of the addition of this new luxury building in the city, but because most people don't usually visit funeral homes just to look around. On this day, they could.

The grand opening with a ribbon cutting and tours was a big event. It featured local officials, including Ormond Beach Mayor David Hood and neighboring Daytona Beach Mayor Bud Asher, along with representatives from the Ormond Beach Chamber of Commerce and the Ormond Beach Historical Society.

Many funeral homes, especially older ones, are shrouded in near-darkness because there are no windows, or very few. Inside Ormond Funeral Home, massive amounts of light poured in from huge windows in the cavernous reception area spanning two stories high, about twenty-seven feet. Stained glass windows line the top portion of the room. Marble floors, plus two giant chandeliers on each end of the reception area reinforced the image of elegance not seen in many, if not most, funeral homes in the United States. A few people even referred to this new building as a "Taj Mahal" of funeral homes. At 10,400 square feet, it was larger than Rockefeller's 9,000 square-foot Casements home. And on the outside, large white columns supported a portico leading to the front doors. Four expensive Medjool Palm trees, along with colorful flowers and lush landscaping also drew attention to this new structure that was hard to miss while traveling the busy street in front of it, Granada Boulevard.

"Nothing is more important to your business than curb appeal," says Lowell.

At fifty-three-years old when he built Ormond Funeral Home, Lowell was like many entrepreneurs in that he had already owned multiple types of businesses – and learned that not all of them prosper at all times. Overall, he had done well, but he still remembered those times when he lost money and racked up debt, primarily during recessions in the 1970s and early 1980s. Though he did not take on business debt willingly, he believed then, and still does now, that wealth cannot be created without debt. From that experience, he learned what he now says was his "first true lesson" in the world of business – and what would also become yet another Lowellism: "Traditionally, every seven or eight years, the economy and stock market will crash. Try to choose a profession or career that is not adversely affected when the economy goes down."

Easier said than done, perhaps. But Lowell had experienced the benefits of being in the cemetery and funeral business even when the economy was not strong.

He has never been involved in the nitty-gritty details of operating a funeral home or cemetery, such as embalming bodies in preparation for a funeral and burial, or cremating remains – or even helping families make funeral arrangements. All that work requires one to be a licensed funeral director. Lowell preferred to hire funeral directors rather than become one himself. It's part of his philosophy in running a business: delegate, delegate, delegate. He is a master at delegating and not getting involved with details. "Anytime you have a job and you have someone who can do it as good as you, and you do it anyway, you just took a step backward," he says.

He felt certain there was a market for this $1.5 million Ormond Funeral Home, which was far more upscale than the three other funeral homes in the city – and even those in adjacent Daytona Beach, or any others in Volusia County or neighboring Flagler County. Volusia Memorial, one of the three existing funeral homes in Ormond Beach, was only about a mile away. Ironically, it was built by Lowell and his family in the 1980s after they purchased what was then called Ormond Memorial Cemetery where Lowell and Victor worked.

Lowell knew the Ormond Beach and Daytona Beach

LOWELL'S INSIGHT

Money
Never forget – cash is king.

---

area very well.

Even though the median household income and the per capita income in Ormond Beach were all considerably higher than Daytona Beach, which had a population nearly double that of Ormond, Lowell still heard that some of his competitors were saying he spent too much money on Ormond Funeral Home.

"I really wanted to bring a first-class funeral home to Ormond Beach. I knew it needed one here. My thinking was, it wasn't all about the money."

Still, Lowell felt sure it would eventually pay off because it made a statement, it established a higher bar for the local funeral business, and it was the foundation for building others and growing a family company.

There also was another reason that entered into his decision to build what he determined would be the nicest funeral home in the area – and it could be said that that reason was not strictly about business. This hard-charging entrepreneur with a passion for business did it in the name of love. He would do anything for Nancy, never mind that she hadn't suggested it. Of course, Lowell was absolutely certain this merging of the personal and business was the perfect union for the couple's future success. And his thinking at the time: "We'd have a great life together."

He would find out soon enough whether residents would embrace the new business or whether they, like some of his competitors, felt the prices would be higher in order to justify this luxurious building. Lowell wasn't concerned. In his mind, with his background and experience, and the sales and business practices he always put into place when he owned funeral homes – and cemeteries – this gave the Lohmans a distinct advantage. He believed the other funeral homes in the area were the ones that should be concerned.

Chapter 10

Beginnings

"Death, like birth, is one of nature's mysteries....
Nothing about death should shame or
upset us, for it is entirely in keeping with our
nature as rational animals and with the law governing us."
Marcus Aurelius

Lowell did what he had always done to generate business. He turned on the marketing machine and put people into positions aimed at generating pre-need sales. He was confident that many people would contact Ormond Funeral Home if they had a death in the family. But he wasn't going to wait for that to happen. He handled much of the pre-need sales himself, and he also brought in Ty to do the same. But that didn't work out initially.

Ty had some experience and from the time he was a child, he wanted to work in the family business. In fact, as a youngster, when he was in the seventh grade, his dad put him to work at the family's cemeteries mowing grass, laying sod and installing vaults. Later, he worked pre-need sales alongside Lowell and his uncle, Victor. He also had sales experience working several summers at Lowell's cemeteries in Atlanta.

"Dad was tough on me, which he had to be because he had to reel me in a couple of times. I needed it because I wasn't quite matured yet," Ty recalls. "But I tell you what, he's the best teacher. I wouldn't be anywhere without him today, that's for sure, and I'm so thankful to have a dad like that, especially for his patience, which back then I don't think I thought he had any. But now when I look back, I realize he was so patient with me. Back then, I thought he was so tough, but you got to be, especially to run a business like this."

Ty left Ormond Funeral Home and went back to Jacksonville where he had previously worked in sales for a large Internet company. But it wasn't long before Lowell asked Ty to come back into the business on Lowell's one condition: become a licensed funeral director. Ty agreed and he went to the same school Nancy had attended. Ty recalls, "If Nancy can do it, I can do it."

In the early days and weeks after the grand opening, not many people were choosing Ormond Funeral Home, aside from the pre-need sales being made. But for at-need service, as it's called when there's been a death in the family and the services of a funeral home are needed, there were only a few calls a month during those first three or four months. It was partly because people assumed that to have a funeral at this grand new place, it would be expensive, although in reality, the prices were competitive with local funeral homes. There also was some confusion about the name, or remembering the name, because there was Volusia Memorial Funeral Home not far away, which was the one Lowell and his family had built and owned years earlier. And, as with any new business, it was not always readily apparent what phone number to call or who to call. In short, these were all temporary branding issues that marketing and time would resolve.

During the first full calendar year of operation, 1999,

the Lohmans conducted approximately one-hundred-fifteen funerals, a pace that was on track to a profitable business. Of course, pre-need sales were ongoing – and those were filling the pipeline for future business.

Nancy took care of meeting and comforting families, making funeral arrangements and conducting funerals. She was the face of the company and provided all the community outreach.

Just as Lowell expected, Nancy was the ideal person to meet with families to arrange funerals.

"That was always the part of funeral directing that came naturally to me because I enjoy hearing people's stories," she says. "I liked hearing about what made their loved one special, and about their family's most treasured memories. I had chosen human ecology as a major, the study of human behavior. I enjoyed it. I always appreciated the gift of being a part of those tender moments with families."

Of course, not all family members planning a funeral got along with one another, or they might not even be speaking to each other, or may not have had contact in years. Now, suddenly, they're together making funeral arrangements for a loved one. Navigating those family dynamics can be a minefield for a funeral director.

Business continued to increase, and during the 2000 calendar year, the Lohmans served about one hundred and fifty families, a number that is generally sufficient to turn a profit. In November of that year, the family purchased Edgewater New Smyrna Cemetery, which was in the southern part of the county, about thirty miles from Ormond Beach. Improvements there commenced immediately, adding more curb appeal, installing new signs, paving roads and more. This was the first property the Lohmans purchased, but Lowell was always on the prowl for other cemeteries and funeral homes even as the volume of business at Ormond Funeral Home continued to rise to approximately two hundred and fifty families served a year.

Lowell also saw the need for a new cemetery in the Ormond Beach-Daytona Beach area, and he began negotiating to purchase thirty acres west of Interstate 95 that cut through both cities. He was considering building a funeral home on that property as well. But state officials had other ideas. Rather than approving Lowell's plans, they preferred he purchase and operate an already existing cemetery, the largest in the area. It was Bellevue-Cedar Hill Memory Gardens, which encompassed ninety acres in the center of Daytona Beach. It included two cemeteries, a funeral home, a crematory and a cremation society. But Bellevue-Cedar Hill was in big trouble. Frequent headlines and stories in the media detailed the problems: botched burials, misplaced and lost bodies, missing baby caskets, allegations that gold teeth were stolen from bodies, unkempt and overgrown grounds, decaying tombstones, and other problems that left families of the deceased angry and demanding answers.

State investigators had been called in. They ousted the owners. Criminal charges were filed. The state took over operations and a court-appointed receiver was placed in charge of managing the business while working to facilitate a sale to a company to resolve the problems and make improvements. Officials in charge of approving new cemeteries, and the receiver who had been appointed, Jim Stephens, urged Lowell and his family to buy the troubled property. They knew if Lowell built the new cemetery he planned, then the problems at Bellevue would be exacerbated and it might never recover.

"I met with Jim and I told him it scares me to death

because if we make a mistake here, our whole family will have to move out of town," Lowell says.

A story in the Daytona Beach News-Journal quoted both Lowell and Nancy expressing their fears about taking on this property.

"We had a good reputation and didn't want to ruin it," Nancy told the newspaper.

"This could be the biggest mistake we could make in our entire lives," Lowell added.

Aside from the scrutiny that would come with being in the public spotlight to right the wrongs, Lowell also knew his family would have to spend hundreds and hundreds of thousands of dollars to rehabilitate and renovate the property, and more to turn it into a first-class sanctuary.

Despite all that, the potential and the possibilities for the cemetery and funeral home campus and what it could be struck Lowell like a giant opportunity. One reason was a treasure trove of information, files containing names of families who had over the years used the funeral home or buried loved ones in the cemetery. Many of these families might choose the funeral home and cemetery again if the property was transformed and operated as it should be.

So, Lowell and his family agreed to buy it.

The price would be $2.1 million, of which $300,000 would be returned to be spent repairing a mausoleum that was in bad shape. Another important part of the deal was that the Lohmans couldn't be sued for any of the previous and existing problems. Additionally, it was contingent on Lowell being released from any legal obligations to purchase the thirty acres along Interstate 95.

One of the very first actions Lowell took was to call his

brother, Victor, and urge him to manage the cemeteries. To Lowell, there was no one better-suited for the job. Victor had many years of experience and the expertise to handle whatever issues might crop up. Victor was essentially retired, spending much of his time on the golf course, but he had read and heard many of the stories about the troubled cemetery. That made him nervous about stepping in to manage it. But he also believed he and Lowell had the experience and expertise to fix it. "Can we straighten everything out? Probably not," he recalls thinking at the time. "But we can make it right from here forward and as best we could, keep correcting anything that needed to be corrected from the past."

He agreed to take the job – and return to work with Lowell and family, albeit with different family members than the first time he and Lowell were in business together. Now it would be Lowell, Nancy, Ty and Victor. Lowell was thrilled to not only have Victor's expertise and years of experience managing cemeteries, but to once again have him in the family business.

Chapter 11

New Life

*"The knowledge of the past is desired
only for the service of the future and the present."*
Friedrich Nietzsche

The Lohmans immediately began cleaning up and restoring Bellevue-Cedar Hill, or as Lowell says, they "attacked it." They resurveyed the cemetery grounds and examined records to determine the extent of the problems regarding bodies buried in the wrong places and remains misplaced or even missing or lost, such as those of a baby boy and two other children. Lowell and Nancy set aside $30,000 to build a monument to the lost infants. The design would come from parents of the three children whose remains were lost. Families were heartbroken and angry that their loved ones hadn't been properly taken care of. It was a gut-wrenching situation.

For what was supposed to be a sanctuary, a place of reverence, the conditions at Bellevue-Cedar Hill were just the opposite. The Lohmans were shocked and somewhat overwhelmed at the magnitude of what they were taking on. The goals were to rectify the problems, help families ease their pain and position the property for the present and future.

Curb appeal, one of the most important features to Lowell, was sorely lacking. The grounds were a mess, in some places overgrown with weeds or simply looking like abandoned property. New landscaping such as hedges and flowers were added, irrigation systems were repaired and expanded, privacy fencing was added around maintenance buildings, surfaces were power-washed and painted, and new granite entrance signs similar to those at Ormond Funeral Home were added.

All of this was done early on. And there would be much, much more to come.

"Small, subtle changes make a huge difference," Lowell told the International Cemetery & Funeral Management magazine.

Victor, the general manager, was quoted as saying, "Every week, families pull in and look up to the hill to the Christus (feature) and tell me that it's just beautiful." The Lohmans had renovated the Christus statue and given it new life.

A new seventeen-foot-tall angel heralding a trumpet and standing on a pedestal graced the entrance. It was a $30,000 synthetic bronze structure aimed at giving visitors an inviting and welcoming arrival. Other statues – features – would be added throughout the grounds of what was no longer Bellevue-Cedar Hill, but now Daytona Memorial Park & Funeral Home. The new name was another sign of a fresh start, a new direction and a way to perhaps help erase some of the bad memories. It also was part of the new owners' marketing efforts. Ormond Funeral Home also would get a new name: Lohman Funeral Home Ormond. Lowell knew there would be opportunities to add more funeral homes and cemeteries under the Lohman family name, and he was beaming with optimism for the family company's growth, in part because with Nancy, Victor and Ty as key members of the business, Lowell's vision of building a company with family was taking shape.

This was only the beginning.

In the early months after the Lohman's took over the Bellevue-Cedar Hill property, the past problems cropped up again when bones were found on the grounds. Media coverage shined an unwanted spotlight. At the cemetery, Lowell was interviewed on camera by a television news reporter. He remembers it well.

"I didn't sugar coat it: 'We found several bones and we're in the process of investigating what they are.' I told them 'the good news was we didn't create the problems, but we were definitely going to correct them....' At that point, we never heard another negative word. I think the interviewer may have expected me to make some kind of excuse for finding the bones, but I said it plain,'" he recalls. "We grew up in this city. I was going to under-promise and over-deliver. That's another Lowellism, by the way. I knew whatever they were expecting, I was doing more."

Lowell also is fond of saying that in business he would rather have "disorganized prosperity than organized poverty." Nancy told him that's exactly what he got when the family purchased Bellevue-Cedar Hill. "It was, behind the scenes, chaotic," she says. "There was so much to do."

She and Victor often reminded each other their job was to bury those who died yesterday in the right space for tomorrow. "Our job is not to fix decades and decades of problems, but when problems arose, it was our job to find the most satisfying solution for that family," she says. "We had to make sure who we were burying was buried in the correct place, absolutely. That was critical, and Victor was good and meticulous about that. That (would be) a huge part of our success at Daytona Memorial – his expertise."

In the southeast corner of the property, Lowell had a vision of what could be after he discovered a lake and wooded area. "I put my Levis on and went back there with the workers as they were clearing and said, 'Boy, this could be something really nice,'" he told the local newspaper.

What he envisioned was a collection of high-end private estate mausoleums situated around the water. A lighted fountain and thirty-foot Medjool Palm trees would add to the ambience. A rock garden and benches could be welcoming features. And, although he may not have had the idea immediately to add two swans to grace the lake that would come to be known as Swan Lake, it was an idea that proved its worth. Their presence would evoke a peaceful and tranquil chord of emotions from visitors. Nancy, Ty and Lowell began calling Victor the "Swan Whisperer" because he taught his staff how to acclimate, manage and care for them.

As appealing and serene as the setting could become for families of loved ones entombed there, Lowell knew the idea of private estates also made sense from a business standpoint. These kinds of mausoleums could sell for anywhere from one-hundred-thousand dollars to perhaps one million dollars. He immediately put his ideas into action.

Also on the agenda were plans for a community mausoleum with four-hundred-fifty crypts for individuals and their loved ones. Additionally, a Cremation Garden and a Veterans Garden featuring more than twenty-one-hundred spaces were planned. A huge American flag would fly in the Veteran's Garden and a memorial with pillars representing each branch of the armed services would be installed. Families could have the names of their loved ones engraved on a platform.

"We planned the new veterans garden with enough spaces that we could offer every veteran in the area a free pre-need burial space and still have spaces available for their spouses and/or other family members," Lowell told the International Cemetery & Funeral Management magazine.

The Lohmans had many other ideas for new services and features to not only restore Daytona Memorial Park, but make it a showplace to be appreciated by the community. A complete makeover, though, would take time – several years and beyond. Behind the scenes, the work was never-ending for the Lohmans. "We were all incredibly busy, keeping everything on track," says Nancy. "There was so much to do, so many administrative and operational protocols, procedures and systems which needed to be implemented."

Even with so much ongoing work, Lowell never lost sight of opportunities to add more funeral homes and cemeteries to the company's holdings. The same year the Lohmans bought Bellevue-Cedar Hill, they acquired Alderson's Funeral Home in Palm Coast, Florida, located in Flagler County just north of Ormond Beach. The location met Lowell's business operating criteria of clustering funeral homes and cemeteries rather than owning properties scattered in Florida or beyond. This one became Lohman Funeral Home Palm Coast.

The idea to have high-end private estate mausoleums – essentially stand-alone buildings with walk-in vestibules – and the surrounding gardens and lake at Daytona Memorial Park immediately captured the attention of several local families. A real estate developer, Edwin Peck, Sr., contacted Lowell almost as soon the Lohmans purchased the property. He and his wife, Hilda, and their family already owned several spaces. They were not only thrilled the Lohmans would transform the place, they became the first to purchase a private estate mausoleum. It had space for six crypts. A story in The New York Times about the trend of estate mausoleums described it:

"A Greek-pillared neo-Classical style structure of white granite, Mr. Peck's mausoleum has a granite patio, a meditation room, doors of handcast bronze and a chandelier. The family name is carved and gilded above a lintel that in the original sales model carried the legend 'Your Name.'"

Funeral industry representatives told the newspaper "six feet up and not six feet under is increasingly the direction in which people want their remains stored when they die."

Of course, the price tag limited the number of purchasers, but for those who didn't mind spending the money, it was their kind of eternity.

"People who are going to be buried here can well afford it, so money is not the issue," Peck told the newspaper. "It's a very pleasant place to be. As pleasant as it could be, considering."

The two swans that called the lake home were named Ed and Hilda in honor of the Peck family.

To showcase the availability of the Swan Lake private estates, Lowell and Nancy sent out twelve-hundred letters and invitations to a catered champagne reception. A Daytona Beach Symphony Quartet entertained guests. An artist's renderings of planned improvements to the grounds were on display. A model private estate mausoleum showed the grandeur of these final resting places. Lowell would not permit anyone to make a purchase during the reception. The event was strictly aimed at introducing the concept to residents. Less than twenty-four hours later, the Lohmans received full payment for one private estate and appointments to meet with other potential buyers.

Six of the fourteen lakeside estates were sold during the first eighteen months. Lowell and Nancy also had purchased one for their family.

"You could call it the ultimate Florida retirement community, a place where residents will spend their post-golden years in idyllic surroundings," reported the International Cemetery & Funeral Management magazine.

Later on, after the Lohmans realized the powerful presence of graceful swans to visitors at Daytona Memorial Park, they donated two swans to Florida Hospital Memorial Medical Center to live in a lake near the facility's Comprehensive Cancer Center. Employees named them Faith and Hope.

Improvements and renovations to the former Bellevue grounds and buildings were continuous. Local residents noticed. They realized this was a new era that required a new trust and a belief that the new owners would do what's right. The Lohmans also were making a name for themselves as a company that was growing – buying local competitors and making plans to build more funeral homes.

In downtown Daytona Beach, only a few miles from Daytona Memorial Park was Baggett & Summers, the oldest funeral home in the area. The owner, Larry Summers, approached the Lohmans to see if they would be interested in purchasing it, according to a newspaper story at the time. Summers liked the idea of a local company continuing to operate the funeral home rather than selling to one of the industry's big companies. "I've had the big guys banging on my doors for years. That didn't appeal to me," he said.

For Lowell, the idea that competitors would approach him was proof that the Lohman family business was moving in the right direction. The Lohmans reached an agreement to purchase Baggett & Summers for $1.5 million. The historic funeral home, established in 1917 as Baggett-Whetherby Funeral Home, was the funeral home called upon to retrieve and prepare John D. Rockefeller's body when he died in 1937. At that time, it was Baggett, Whetherby & McIntosh Company. Among its documents when the Lohmans purchased it was Rockefeller's Funeral Record, a large page, perhaps twelve inches by seventeen inches, listing all the vital and official information about Rockefeller at the time of his death. Nancy scanned it for archival purposes, redacted confidential or sensitive information and then had the document framed with archival glass and placed on a wall inside Lohman Funeral Home Ormond amidst other Rockefeller memorabilia and Ormond Beach historical items.

The Lohmans also envisioned having a new 8,000 square-foot funeral home in Port Orange, which was only a few miles south of Daytona Memorial Park. Lowell purchased nearly two-and-a-half acres to build a facility, but during the permitting process, plans changed and construction costs rose. So, the decision was made to sell the property and purchase a building, which would be renovated to become Lohman Funeral Home Port Orange. The land sale netted $400,000.

Cardwell & Maloney Funeral Home in Port Orange and DeLand Memorial Gardens cemetery in nearby DeLand also became properties of the Lohmans when they purchased both from a Houston-based company. At the time of the purchase, Lowell told the local newspaper, "They are all part of our goal to use economies of scale, to cluster locations, to provide the best competitive price." It also eliminated a competitor. The new name: Cardwell Lohman Funeral Home Port Orange.

At Daytona Memorial Park, the continuing

improvements meant demolishing the forty-year-old cemetery administration building and replacing it – and renovating the exterior and interior of the funeral home on the property. Both buildings would be similar in appearance to Lohman Funeral Home Ormond with the gray-colored stucco, white banding and porticos supported by stately white columns.

Among other new features at the cemetery was the installation of a granite and bronze Police and Firefighters Monument listing the names of men and women who died in the line of duty. It was dedicated during the Volusia and Flagler Annual Law Enforcement Memorial Service for each local municipality's police officers and firefighters. Separately, the Lohmans later donated a black onyx statue at the Daytona Beach Police Department's new headquarters. The Daytona Beach Fallen Officers Monument lists the names of Daytona Beach Police Department officers who lost their lives in service. A "Policeman's Prayer" is engraved on one side of the monument.

The Lohmans considered adding a pet cemetery, separate but adjacent to Daytona Memorial Park, and the more they explored the idea, the more they realized it made sense to offer families services and burial or cremation for their pets. At the same time, Lowell and Nancy were thinking about their own cat, Stretch, and where he would be interred when the time came. Stretch, a rescue from the Halifax Humane Society who was now thought to be about thirteen years old, was struggling with his health and had been receiving dialysis twice a week for about two years to treat kidney failure.

The Lohmans selected two acres on the grounds, secured the necessary state permits and designed a pet cemetery, as well as a private pet crematory in a separate building.

The most prominent feature of the pet cemetery was the

seventeen-foot statue of an angel petting a dog on one side and a cat on the other. It was built of fiberglass and painted bronze, and sits atop the columbarium. But the Lohmans designed it so it could be removed and used at expos or in parades. "...You would not believe the buzz she has created for us. Thousands of people have had their photos taken in front of her," Nancy told the funeral industry's ICCFA Magazine. "I cannot tell you how many people have called us to serve their families because of how we took care of their pets. Because of the number of preneed and at-need referrals we've received on the human side, we would consider the pet business a success by that measure alone.

Lowell's appetite for growing the company by buying or building new funeral homes, or buying new cemeteries, seemed unlimited, although in the twelve years since building and opening Ormond Funeral Home in 1998 – now called Lohman Funeral Home Ormond – the Lohman Family Properties company was running out of locations to buy in the two-county area where Lowell preferred to concentrate the business. The company dominated the market. In fact, with its latest purchase – Constantino Funeral Home in DeLand, which was changed to Lohman Funeral Home DeLand – the Lohmans had become the largest private family-owned operator of funeral homes and cemeteries in Florida. "That's something we're very proud of," Lowell said in a 2010 story in the Volusia/Flagler Business Report newspaper featuring the top private companies in Volusia and Flagler counties. The Lohman's company now had thirteen locations and one-hundred-and-twenty-nine employees. The previous year – 2009 – its sales reached $10 million, the most it had ever recorded in a single year.

Nancy was quoted in the story as saying the company's success in large part was because of the clustering of locations in two counties and the operational advantages that come with that. "We share vehicles and can get to any of our locations within 45 minutes," she said. "Our efficiencies in running our business are better than if we only had one or two locations and we're also able to share advertising costs." Additionally, she said Lohman Funeral Homes could compete on price with any competitors locally or even properties owned by the national

> **LOWELL'S INSIGHT**
>
> **Teamwork**
> All successful companies have a culture of teamwork, and we try to promote that every chance we can. I can't recall ever having a monthly or quarterly meeting where I didn't focus on that.

chains.

In the Business Report, Lowell as the company's president and CEO, reiterated his long-used strategy – indeed, his requirement – of focusing on pre-need sales as another of the reasons the company had enjoyed so much success. Those sales accounted for forty percent of the revenue. Nancy, the company's chief operating officer who oversaw all the funeral homes, added: "Sales to families who preplan and therefore predetermine that we are their choice for funeral and/or burial services are what ensures our future." Victor Lohman, vice president and general manager of the cemetery division of the company, was quoted as saying, "By preplanning, it eliminates families from within 24-48 hours of losing a loved one having to go select a casket or walk around a cemetery" to select a burial site. Ty Lohman served as vice president in charge of pre-need sales for all of the company's funeral homes and cemeteries, and managed the large sales force.

The four Lohmans worked well together – and they had done so as the company had grown. Of course, they didn't always agree on various matters, but they could have discussions, and even in disagreement, they empathized with each other.

"What I always said as to why it worked for our family is we each had our own sandbox," says Nancy. "Ty was in charge of pre-need sales, I was over funeral homes, Victor was over cemeteries, and Lowell was our CEO, visionary and cheerleader. He was the umbrella and 'our glue', but it always worked because we each had so much to do within our own divisions that no one could micromanage the other."

"At the end of the day, we're all good friends," says Ty. "We had issues just like everyone else, but we knew at the end of the day, we all had each other's backs. We were all a part of the same goal, and were partners. If I had a problem, I could go to Uncle Victor or Nancy or my dad. I was lucky that I had the three of them to go to."

Lowell was overseeing it all, but not as a micromanager, which certainly worked to his advantage. He was prescient in his vision back in 1996 that Nancy would be the perfect person to be a funeral director and to manage the company's funeral homes. In addition, Nancy says, "It was ideal having Ty manage the heart-beat of the company – its Pre-need Sales Division, and having Victor with his cemetery operations expertise manage the Cemetery Division."

All of this meant Lowell could focus on the big picture of the business, growing and expanding the company.

The Lohmans also implemented what they called "inquiry call phone monitoring." Many families call multiple funeral homes prior to choosing one when they have an imminent death in their family. Lowell could easily determine what funeral directors were telling people who called to inquire about services. They hired people posing as potential customers to make calls, and recorded them. What the funeral directors sometimes said, or didn't say, often resulted in the funeral home getting the business – or not.

The use of phone shoppers was a near constant practice of Lowell's as a way to monitor what funeral directors and pre-need sales counselors were telling potential customers – and more importantly, to him, to help employees correct the problems. The phone shopping, of course, was part of Lowell's "systems and monitoring."

Nancy was the executive overseeing funeral directors at each of the Lohman's various properties. She put into place systems to monitor customer satisfaction, and procedures and policies aimed at "excellent" funeral services. "Best practice ideas" were continually implemented. Training, including role-playing, was ongoing.

"I was very big on systems and monitoring because I learned that from Lowell. We always had a guideline for funeral arrangement conferences, and then we had a very important checklist for the kinds of things that we made sure were done for every funeral service. I coined the term, non-negotiable, for certain things. There were certain things that we had to do for every single family, for every single service. Some of those helped set the Lohman Funeral Homes apart from their competitors, and helped with branding the Lohman business," she says. "I was very proud of our staff and the funeral services they provided."

Nancy established strict procedures and policies for cremation because a simple mistake could have huge consequences. "If I were asked what would keep me up at night, it was anything to do with cremation because it's so non-reversible. The liability is huge, so you have to have the systems in place to make sure every detail and all the logistics are handled professionally and properly."

Nancy always wanted funerals to be perfect for families. It was difficult for her to not be involved in details.

"It was hard for me to let go, unlike Lowell who was really good at delegating. I'm not so good at that because I just wanted things to be so right for the families we served. I think I probably created a lot more work for myself, but it was so rewarding when we were a part of a beautiful funeral or tribute. It was rewarding when a family would tell me they couldn't imagine a better funeral service for their loved one. I can't imagine a better compliment than that, and we got those a lot. When we would, on occasion, disappoint a family, it took me a long time to process it even though I tried to resolve it immediately as best I could."

Nancy's background in the hospitality management business and in coordinating events also fit well in the funeral business where she was helping families make arrangements and creating "celebrations of life." Additionally, with her business background, she envisioned and implemented changes to the funeral homes to better meet the needs of families. For example, she created reception and banquet areas because more and more people wanted catering services, or at least a place where everyone could gather and have food and drinks before or after a service. "Where do we all gather in our homes during celebrations? The kitchen. When do we bring all our families together? For a holiday meal like Thanksgiving," she says. "When we break bread together, it creates a connection, so I created a reception area at every funeral home. It wasn't easy because they weren't always designed physically for those areas, but we created them as best we could. I knew that was an important way to keep our funeral homes relevant. I worried about staying relevant because things were changing in our industry due to changing customer preferences. People needed to know they could come to our funeral home and have everything or anything they wanted."

Over time, more and more people asked to "personalize" the funeral of their loved one, creating a tribute that often revolved around a theme such as golf or surfing or some other aspect of life that had been important to the person whose funeral was being conducted.

"Our job was to do what the family wanted," says Lowell. "If they wanted helicopters dropping flower petals on the cemetery, we did it. We had dove and balloon releases. We arranged for bagpipers and musicians. We bent over backwards, same as everyone else in the industry, to make them happy. We had tributes for surfers and our funeral directors arranged paddle-out services at the beach. We even drove processions down the beach so families could share one more day at the ocean together. Golfers? We've had their golf bags and putters." For some, fishing was their passion and that was the theme of the funeral.

On many occasions, the Lohmans conducted funerals for bikers – motorcyclists – whose families opted to have their loved one transported in the "Harley Hearse" the Lohmans had custom-built for just this reason. "There are tons of bikers in Daytona," says Lowell. The black Harley-Davidson motorcycle was a police motorcycle transformed into a three-wheeled machine. It pulled the wooden hearse manufactured by a carriage firm. The Lohmans also offered families the use of a

1939 antique Pontiac hearse or a traditional hearse.

Of course, Nancy, as the funeral director and the person overseeing funeral directors, was the person most responsible for helping families add personalization to funerals. She invested in celebrant training for herself and all her funeral directors. It was a week-long off-site training program conducted by industry colleagues Doug Manning and Glenda Stansbury of the InSight Institute along with independent funeral home owners Ernie Heffner and Mark Krause. The training helped funeral directors learn how to more fully customize and personalize tributes and life celebrations. "Funeral directors now needed to think of themselves as event planners," says Nancy. "Those who don't embrace this will struggle in the future."

"Whether it was a service, a party or a celebration of life, to a degree it was challenging work to create an elaborate event in a short timeframe. For families, the cultural change was a healthy change. They wanted to remember their loved one's life with a celebration or a special ceremonial element of some kind with keepsakes, memorabilia and photo presentations. I loved coordinating all that," she says. "I would encourage all of our funeral directors to search for ways to create some kind of take-away gift to provide at the end of the service. They didn't have to be expensive, they just needed to speak to the passion of the person who died."

Lowell and Ty frequently had pre-need sales counselors attend the funeral arrangement conference so they could meet the family. Many funeral directors didn't like that, but funeral directors were not likely to be the person following up later with a family to discuss pre-planning their own funeral. The sales counselor – family service counselor – could do that. This was another way Lowell and Ty kept a focus on pre-need sales.

"We always wanted to analyze what separated us from our competitors," Lowell says. "Every funeral home has people who take good care of the families. We like to believe that nobody did as good a job as we did, but the other funeral homes were doing a good job, too. We like to believe that our facilities were better than theirs, but most of their facilities were good, also. So, to me, that was not what separated us. Our involvement in the community was an advantage that we had over our competitors, but that's not the biggest advantage. The biggest advantage we had over our competitors was two words: pre-need sales. That's what drove our company. It's not inherent in the competitors' personalities. It's not something they like. They hate pre-need sales, and we thrived on it. We would not be as big as we were in the funeral business without the pre-need sales. Most funeral homes are sitting there waiting for somebody to call, and that's when they do business. The Lohmans were aggressive. The last thing that a funeral home anywhere wanted to hear is the Lohmans just bought the competitor across the road from them because we are bringing in telemarketers, we're increasing the advertising, and training our people to get out and meet people. It makes so much sense to do it ahead of time. When you analyze the funeral business, that's what you have to do. The average person thinks we're sitting behind the desk waiting for someone to come in. I don't think anybody in our industry attacked pre-need sales like we did. We did more volume every month in pre-need sales than we ever did in at-need sales."

Lowell also kept an eye on the big picture, always looking to add more properties such as he did in 2011 when the company built Lohman Funeral Home Deltona, not far from DeLand where the Lohmans already owned a funeral home and cemetery. Lohman Family Properties now had a total of 14 locations.

As the CEO and president, Lowell wasn't involved in the day-to-day operations. He liked to pretend he was hovering in a helicopter, seeing all that was going on without getting directly involved in too many details. That didn't mean he was hands-off, though. He sometimes likened himself to a "fire-breathing dragon" on those occasions when he saw problems with people or policies. It wasn't so much that he was angry, but rather determined and intense when he delivered his messages. Afterward, in those situations when he had leveled criticism, he says he always tried to remember to "rescue" the employee, leaving him or her with something positive, a message that illustrated the "warmth" and the caring-about-the-person part of the "power and warmth" philosophy he believes is necessary for a leader.

There also was a lot of "teaching and sharing," says Nancy.

"He truly would bring everyone together, all of us together as a family, all of the team together as a company. It was really important to him to teach and share, but along with that, he always said, 'My family runs each part of the business and I don't do a thing.' He would joke about that. We all knew that wasn't true. He took his role seriously as our visionary and our cheerleader, but also understood what was important in each division of our business," she says.

"One of the analogies we used was he would soar like an eagle above us, and then he would just dive down into our ponds. I called them sandboxes. He would dive down into our ponds and grab you, and you'd just be floppy like a fish in the claws of an eagle. But he'd only dive into your pond if you deserved it," she adds.

"You always knew he was not only very strong, but he was always right. He was also always decent. That's why someone early on in business coined the phrase 'decent boldness wins respect' when referring to Lowell. That wasn't something he walked around saying. When (he and his family) sold their funeral homes and cemeteries in 1989, that phrase was presented to him on a thank-you plaque. It was a phrase that was used to describe Lowell that he didn't come up with. It was all of his associates who said decent boldness wins respect. Lowell is

> NANCY'S INSIGHT
>
> **Customer Service**
> Remember the Sunset Rule: Don't put off addressing any issue that could result in a lack of customer satisfaction. Take care of it before you leave for the day. Don't put it off until tomorrow and then have an even bigger issue.

always bold, but decent."

For Nancy, recognizing and understanding Lowell's role in the business, her own role, and those of Victor and Ty, were keys to having successful relationships in running a family business.

"I really think I sensed that he was the boss, our CEO and president, and I had a lot to learn from him. He proved all the time that he was 'spot-on'. Sometimes when you get your toes stepped on, when you're not doing the job as well as you should be, it hurt. It was frustrating not doing a great job all the time because every one of us wanted to do a great job. It's a part of life and a part of the professional world to have to accept feedback and learn from it. Lowell always had a way of coming back to save you."

Lowell never believed in keeping an employee in a job if that employee was not meeting expectations or not improving. For example, if two sales counselors had been on the job for six months, and they were not selling, Lowell would tell the person in charge to "let them go so they can go somewhere else to make a living."

Lowell and Ty's strategy for hiring new pre-need sales counselors was at times a bit unconventional. Job applicants calling in response to a newspaper ad by the funeral home or cemetery would be asked if they could come in for an interview within the next few hours. They weren't interested in the applicant sending a resume and waiting days to have an opportunity to interview. Lowell and Ty wanted to see how much urgency they had for a job, how enthusiastic they were, and how they would adapt to this unexpected situation of being asked to come in immediately.

Other times, when there was already a list of names of applicants who had called in, Lowell would call every one of them on a Sunday evening and asked that they come in Monday morning for an interview.

"That lobby would be full," Nancy says. "He'd fill the sales boardroom up with (prospective) pre-need sales counselors – and Tuesday, we'd have eight new employees."

Once, Nancy couldn't believe what Lowell did when one man came in to apply for a pre-need sales position. "He was in jeans, boots, bandana, tattoos everywhere; this is clearly not someone who understands the scope of a professional business they are walking into. He's not someone you'd have meet with families, from first looking at him. He obviously, from his looks, didn't have a sense for how you dress for an interview when you're not sure what you're walking into. Overdress in a professional manner instead of underdress. I thought this was going to be a five-minute interview with Lowell. So, two hours later, the guy comes out and leaves. I asked Lowell why he had been with him so long. He said if he didn't spend those two hours with him, nobody would have. He said, 'I'm the only one who would have invested in that guy for two hours, and he needed to talk about a lot of things.' I'm sure Lowell spent a lot of time coaching on, not just what our business was about, but how to dress for an interview. He invested time into somebody when most people, including myself, would not have."

The man wasn't hired, but Lowell hoped the advice he gave would help the man in his next job interview.

For Nancy, it was another example of her learning from Lowell something new related to one aspect of running a business, about having respect for every single person.

"I know we have influenced each other. Lowell has made me a better businessperson. He has helped me to be able to look at a lot of different aspects of business. Before I was in business with Lohman Family Properties, I knew what a financial statement was, but I probably didn't understand it like I do. I didn't understand some of the business philosophies such as buying down debt as you go along. Just different things that I do as second nature now, with the help of Lowell's 'teach and share' support."

The four family members, Lowell, Nancy, Victor and Ty each had ownership in the company, and even though they got along well, business discussions, arguments and disagreements could occasionally be intense. "But at the end of the day, we always circled back," says Nancy. "The person who was too strong, whether right or wrong, would apologize. We always knew it was important to circle back as a family. None of us were too big to apologize."

The growth and success of this family-owned company, which by the nature of its business was very much in the public eye, caught the attention of the Family Business Center at Stetson University in DeLand. The center's director, Greg McCann, visited with the Lohmans to see how such a family business could work, given the various roles and interests and age differences of individual family members. Lowell owned forty percent of the company, and Nancy, Victor and Ty each owned twenty percent. They had not had to buy into the business. Instead, Lowell believed that giving partial ownership to the family members working in the business was simply the right thing to do. It also was tangible evidence of Lowell's belief that Nancy, Victor and Ty were the three best people to be in the top positions. In 2012, as Lowell looked back at the progress and success the company had enjoyed since building and opening Ormond Funeral Home in 1998, their roles were further proof of the importance of having the right people in the right positions.

Together, the family had built an extremely valuable company. Other funeral home and cemetery companies saw what the Lohmans had achieved – and several of them, especially the publicly traded companies, wanted to buy Lohman Family Properties. This was a coveted company – fourteen properties all located in a two-county area in the state of Florida, a mecca for an increasing number of retirees who would need funeral, burial or cremation services when their final day arrived. The Lohmans had become the largest private family-owned company of funeral homes and cemeteries in Florida.

Lowell at the K-9 Statue unveiling at Lohman Pet Cemetery adjacent to Daytona Memorial Park in 2009.

Lohman Funeral Home Daytona

Family members, left to right, Daryl Lohman, Lowell Lohman, Opal Lohman Silverman, Victor Lohman and Irv Silverman representing their company, Sloman Enterprises, in 1996.

Lohman Funeral Home Ormond

Lohman family Private Estate Mausoleum at Daytona Memorial Park.

Swans Ed and Hilda in Swan Lake within the Private Estates section in Daytona Memorial Park.

An advertisement for Lohman Funeral Homes.

Lowell and Nancy, 2006. Photo used with permission of *The Daytona Beach News-Journal*.

The Lohman family members who owned Lohman Family Properties (funeral homes and cemeteries). From left to right, Victor, Nancy, Lowell and Ty, in 2009.

The Private Estates section in Daytona Memorial Park.

The Cremation Garden at Swan Lake in Daytona Memorial Park.

The Lohmans, left to right, Ty, Victor, Nancy and Lowell at Lohman Pet Cemetery adjacent to Daytona Memorial Park.

Lowell and Nancy present their initial donation to the Halifax Humane Society at the 2016 Fur Ball. Ultimately, they increased their gift to a total of $1 million.

Like father, like son. Ty and Lowell in 2006.

The closing for the $25 million sale of Lohman Family Properties in 2012. Lowell, Nancy, Ty and Victor with their attorney Jeff Brock, seated.

Ty, Lowell and Nancy at the corporate office of their company, Lohman Apartments - Eagle Properties, 2016.

Lowell, Nancy, and Ty on Dock of one of the properties they owned, Eagle Bay Apartments.

Lowell and Ty in the Club House of
Eagle Bay Apartments.

Ty, Nancy and Lowell at one of the apartment buildings they owned. Photo used with permission of *The Daytona Beach News-Journal*.

Wedding photo, Lowell and Nancy, 1991.

Nancy and Lowell with Snowball.

Nancy was crowned 1981 Homecoming Queen at Ohio State University.

Nancy and Lowell and friends at the 35th Homecoming Reunion Parade at Ohio State University in 2016. Pictured are Nancy and Lowell, Ty Lohman, Bill Stephens, Roy Gailey, Sherry Gailey, Bridget Bergens, Jill Stephens, Laurentia Lucas, Victor Lohman, Jill Simpkins, Lorry Hood, Mary McAree, Susan Persis and Nan Heebner.

Lowell and Nancy's home in Ormond Beach, Florida.

At Machu Picchu, 2007.

At the Taj Mahal in India, 2007.

In Antarctica in 2017.

At Hawaii Keck Observatory at Mauna Kea on the big island, Hawaii, in 2002. Lowell has long had an interest in astronomy.

At Lowell's 70th birthday in 2015, friends gathered at Oceanside Country Club in Ormond Beach for a party and the opportunity to roast Lowell, seated in the gold chair. Pictured with him are Christopher Lohman, Daryl Lohman, Bryan Collyer, Roy Gailey, Ken Nichols, Ty Lohman, Carl Persis, Edgar Scott and Bill Stephens.

Lowell and Nancy.

Chapter 12

'Every Business Has a Moment'

"I like things to happen: and if they don't happen, I like to make them happen."
Winston Churchill

In 2012, the fourteen Lohman family businesses – eight funeral homes, four cemeteries and two crematories – were continuing to make money. Business was good despite some strong headwinds in the industry. And even though several potential buyers of the company were circling, Lowell wasn't focused on the idea of selling. His mindset was always to grow by buying or building new properties. He considered expanding into other cities west of Volusia County, including Orlando, because the Lohmans already dominated the markets in their home county, Volusia, and Flagler County to the north. But Lowell knew the winds of change in the funeral and cemetery industry were picking up speed – and they were blowing in the wrong direction, away from traditional funerals and cemetery burials, and toward cremation. The Lohmans were experiencing it in their businesses.

When families chose to have their loved ones cremated, that drastically affected profits of funeral homes and cemeteries. Cremations, which are inexpensive compared with funerals or burials in a cemetery, do not produce much revenue. The long-standing business model used in the death-care industry was simply no longer a good fit for the new choices and demands of consumers.

Early on, cremations comprised about thirty-five percent of the Lohmans' business, but now, about seventy percent of the families chose cremation, sometimes without having a funeral or celebration of life service or choosing to place the cremated remains at the cemetery.

Of course, the reason many families were choosing cremation was simply because they didn't have to spend as much money. Some families whose religious beliefs didn't prevent them from considering cremation also were choosing to forego the traditional funeral or burial in a cemetery. Nancy always encouraged the funeral directors at Lohman Funeral Homes to make sure families knew that even with cremation, they could still have other services. "I told our staff to go up to bat three times. Try three times to help them understand the myriad choices and services they could arrange at Lohmans to

> ### NANCY'S INSIGHT
>
> **Pay Business Mortgages Quickly**
> Lowell taught us to have a mortgage with a lower finite number of years. So, get an eight or ten or fifteen-year mortgage and release yourself from that debt sooner rather than later. Alleviate a lot of that interest payment by having that shorter mortgage term.
>
> We had debt, but we were paying down $1 million every year, which meant our businesses were getting more valuable and our cash flow was getting better. We were going to be able to pay ourselves more, eventually, than we were, and we'd probably be able to sleep better.

celebrate and pay tribute to the life of their loved one.

"Personally, I focused a lot on how we could stay relevant in the future with cremation rising like it was, and with direct disposers or storefront funeral homes popping up everywhere," she says. "It was why Lowell convinced me that this was the perfect time to sell because every business has a moment. The one thing he said – I'll never forget – he said, 'Our businesses will never be more valuable than they are now.'"

And, of course, one of his Lowellisms, one of his guiding principles, is: "Sometimes businesses change. You must change with them."

All of the Lohmans – Lowell, Nancy, Victor and Ty – agreed the time was right.

Having been in the business more than three decades, the Lohmans personally knew most of the industry's executives with the large companies that coveted family-owned businesses like the Lohmans'. Nancy also knew the top industry officials and she herself was known because she had long served on the board of directors and was now president-elect of the International Cemetery, Cremation and Funeral Association, the world's oldest and largest trade group serving the industry. Additionally, she had been president of the Southern Cemetery, Cremation and Funeral Association. Plus, she was active in the Florida Cemetery, Cremation and Funeral Association and the Independent Funeral Directors of Florida. She often was a speaker at various conventions and conferences in the death-care industry. Ty was on the board of the Florida Cemetery, Cremation and Funeral Association, and was in line to become the state association's president in two years.

The Lohmans were well-known in the industry.

In April of 2012, they put together a color portfolio

featuring photos, information and data about each of their properties. This would serve as their calling card, or in reality, their response, because executives of companies interested in purchasing the Lohman properties were in pursuit. To ensure a smooth process and command the highest price, Lowell decided to invite companies to submit bids – and he set a relatively quick deadline.

"We put it out to bid to five. We said if we didn't get at least $23 million dollars, we're not selling," Lowell says. "So, of the first four, two of them were better than twenty and the other two were in the teens."

> *LOWELL'S INSIGHT*
>
> **Negotiating**
> When buying or selling a business or property, it is extremely important that you understand the process and how to negotiate. At an early age, I learned the only way to be sure you had the best prices was to negotiate until you lost it, and then go back and get it. The best transactions are where there's a win-win.

The fifth offer was better than the others.

StoneMor Partners, L.P. bid $23.5 million. At the time, StoneMor, a publicly traded company, was the third largest in the industry, and owned two-hundred and seventy-five cemeteries and sixty-nine funeral homes in twenty-six states, plus Puerto Rico. At dinner with the StoneMor executive handling acquisitions, each of the Lohman partners knew what this offer meant: they would be selling – and they each knew what their percentage of the sale was worth. Even after paying off the relatively low debt the company had, each partner would make millions of dollars. Ty, who owned twenty percent of the company, had tears of joy in his eyes, though no one but him knew that at the time.

Lowell told the StoneMor executive that instead of $23.5 million, he preferred a round number, and that they would have a deal if StoneMor increased its offer to $25 million. The StoneMor executive asked the Lohmans to give him thirty minutes so he could make a call to his bosses – and he really did not want the Lohman family members to leave yet. When he returned, he didn't come back with a different figure. They had a deal for $25 million.

On June 14, the Daytona Beach News-Journal reported in a front-page story that the Lohmans had signed a letter of intent to sell Lohman Family Properties to StoneMor, a company that had generated $228 million in revenue the previous year.

Lowell was quoted as saying the sale also would be beneficial for the Lohman's one-hundred-twenty-one employees. Nancy added that employees would receive increased health care benefits and have "more opportunities for advancement." After the sale closed on July 31, the Lohman's distributed $50,000 to "thank all of their employees for their years of hard work and dedication," says Nancy.

Local residents wouldn't notice much difference in the funeral homes and cemeteries because they would still carry the Lohman name, and Nancy, Victor and Ty agreed to work for the new owners in essentially the same, but expanded positions they previously held. Lowell would retire – mostly. Entrepreneurs like Lowell never really retire. But the next chapter of business for Lowell hadn't yet arrived.

During the Lohmans' fourteen years in business, it was Nancy who personified the brand of Lohman-owned funeral homes and cemeteries. She was the face of the company. This had been an intentional business strategy of Lowell's early on – and he had it in mind even before he asked Nancy to become a funeral director. She and her team would come to be recognized and loved by hundreds and hundreds of families she and her funeral directors helped with funeral arrangements. She also was well-known in the community because of her involvement and leadership in numerous local organizations, including the Ormond Beach Chamber of Commerce (serving two years as President), Ormond Beach Historical Society (serving two terms as President), Ormond Memorial Art Museum and Gardens, Florida Hospital Advisory Board, the Halifax Humane Society and other civic and charitable groups. Her profile and standing in the community and in the Lohman businesses added value – real dollars – to the sale of Lohman Family Properties. One StoneMor executive, Lowell recalls, said having Nancy continue as part of the business could be worth as much as $1 million to $2 million.

Nancy's role expanded with StoneMor to include facilitating acquisitions of other independent funeral homes and cemeteries as Director of Corporate Development reporting to the Executive Vice President of Business Development, Gregg Strom. Gregg had known the Lohman family for decades. It was Gregg whom the Lohmans called at StoneMor when it was time to sell.

Nancy remained with StoneMor for nearly five years and finally left so she could devote more time to other pursuits. Those included completing her graduate degree, a Master of Arts in Leadership Communication from Gonzaga University in May 2017, and traveling the globe with Lowell. The couple loves to travel. After a trip to Antarctica in February 2017, they have been to all seven continents in the world. But there are still plenty of places to see. As Lowell says about Nancy: "She hasn't been everywhere, but it's on her list." They both believe what Lowell's mother was fond of saying about travel: "The anticipation is as much fun as the event." Lowell even has two Lowellisms about the couple's travels: "A happy wife is a happy life," and "Travel is the only thing you buy that makes you richer."

When the Lohman's sale to StoneMor was completed, Victor was named Regional Cemetery Operations Director for Florida, a position he held for StoneMor for several years before retiring. Leading up to that point, Nancy says Victor "had transformed Daytona Memorial Park to the premier cemetery in Volusia while also managing the operations of the other Lohman cemetery properties."

Ty's role with StoneMor was as Regional Vice President of Sales, overseeing pre-need sales at cemeteries in seven states. But even before the Lohmans sold their company, Ty had embarked on a new part-time venture. He saw opportunities in real estate, which had been hit hard by the recession that began in 2008. Recovery was still coming slowly to the housing industry. Ty started buying houses, townhomes and condos – most of them in foreclosure. He renovated and leased them. Most of this was done using $40,000 he inherited after the 2010 death of his grandmother, Opal Silverman, Lowell's mother.

When the Lohmans completed the sale of their funeral homes and cemeteries, Ty had more money to work with. Within a month or so, he bought three apartment complexes, each between $1 million and $2 million. And then more. Less than four months after having received his money from the sale of the funeral homes and cemeteries, it was almost all gone, invested in apartment complexes totaling about 160 units. After some renovations, he began selling, making a tidy profit on each one. Plus, he still had income from the ten properties he first purchased, and he had a couple hundred thousand dollars coming in from his position with StoneMor. Continuing to work in that job provided a bit of a security cushion, and bought him some time, as he got more and more involved in the real estate business. "I stayed on to make sure what I thought I was seeing was what I was seeing," he says.

He learned about several apartment buildings totaling 600 units in the Daytona Beach area that were either in foreclosure or about to be. It would likely take $15 million to $20 million to purchase those. Although he had what he called "serious money" after selling his other properties, it wouldn't be enough to take on this deal. So, he asked his dad if he would be interested in investing. "I told him I was crushing these things, and letting him know the prices were really good," says Ty.

For five days, Ty called and left messages for the representative from a New York bank that was handling the sales of these properties. Finally, on the sixth day, the bank official called him back. "He said he was going to the airport and he'd be there for an hour," says Ty. "So, I called my Dad. He got ready real quick and we went down to see the guy. Dad asked if these were good deals, and I said they were great deals. I said we'd be getting these for less than what I paid for mine, the six I had bought and flipped. So, I said these are great deals, but you're talking about $18 million."

Lowell had never considered investing in the apartment business, but he had watched Ty, and he was impressed with what his son had accomplished and how well he understood the business. "Ty had become a great businessman," he says. For Lowell, nearly seventy years old at the time, the entrepreneurial fires still burned. The competitiveness of building businesses had never gone away even though he no longer felt he needed to prove anything to himself or anyone else. He liked building companies and his passion for business had not slowed. This would also be an opportunity to be in business with his son, in a new Lohman family business. Plus, retirement to Lowell was like wearing a suit that didn't fit. It never felt right. He also didn't particularly like having most of his money in the stock market since the sale of the Lohman Family Properties. Lowell had come to believe that most stockbrokers and financial advisors had "major conflicts of interest" and charged exorbitant fees with advice that seemed to him to be "smoke and mirrors and self-serving." After investing millions of dollars with several brokers, and tracking returns and fees, Lowell determined he and Nancy were better off taking that money and putting it into the Vanguard Standard and Poor's 500 Index Fund – and leaving it alone. The couple's safety net, he says, is apartments. "If the economy goes bad, construction decreases, foreclosures increase, people cannot get loans. Where do they go? Apartments."

The banker handling the sale of the large group of apartments in Daytona Beach was preparing to leave town, but he met with Ty and Lowell. After that, they drove to look at the apartment complexes. They knew if they had a shot at this deal, they would have to move quickly because real estate agents would be trying to get the listing and other buyers and investors would be circling.

"So, we called him, and we said, 'we looked at them and we'll give you $15 million,'" says Lowell. "He said that wouldn't do it, and we hung up. I distinctly remember this: I turned to Ty and I asked him how badly he wanted these apartments. He told me the chance of us finding this many apartments in our backyard at this price may never happen again in Daytona. He was one hundred percent correct. We called the man back. We agreed to give him $17 million and not one penny more. I remember saying not one penny more. We'll give you $17 million and we'll wire a deposit of $1 million in the morning, and he said, 'OK, why don't we do this? I need both of your financial statements, and send them to me so I can look at them, and you have to give me a couple of days.' Well, obviously, within an hour our financial statements were going up to New York. Three days went by and he called to say 'we'll get it started.' That was the

> ## LOWELL'S INSIGHT
>
> ### 'Helicoptering'
>
> I'm looking at the big picture of the business, hovering in what I call my helicopter, and I'm not involved in the details. I live in that helicopter.
>
> I think I have a pretty good feel of what not to get involved in because if I ever get involved too much, and managers and others see that, then guess what happens? They think that's an open door to call and get me involved. If I handle it, and solve it for them, they're going to continue to call me and not solve problems on their own or call their manager for help.
>
> If you're going to grow a decent-sized company, that's not the way to do it. You have to have channels of command, and you've got to stick with them.

moment."

Ty and Lowell discussed the deal and decided Ty would own fifty percent of the business, and Lowell and Nancy would own fifty percent even though they were putting up more money than Ty.

Lowell wanted Ty to be the "front person." "I told him

'I'd do it under one condition, we're fifty-fifty partners. I've seen what a great businessperson you are.' We made a deal that when any cash was generated out of the businesses, his half came to Nancy and I first to pay us back. I couldn't believe that within a year, he had paid us in full. We have been dollar for dollar ever since."

Just as the Lohmans had grown their funeral home and cemetery businesses, they wasted no time buying more apartment complexes. Their strategy also was similar in that they wanted to concentrate the businesses in a limited geographical area: Daytona Beach and other cities in Volusia County, and in Orlando and Jacksonville. "They run better with the economies of scale by being clustered together," says Lowell.

By mid-2014, they had invested $32 million buying nine apartment complexes with 1,173 units in Daytona Beach and Orlando. During the next year, they continued their buying spree, purchasing apartments in Orlando and seven in Jacksonville. By this time, they had invested $119 million and owned seventeen apartment complexes with about 3,700 units.

They also had planned to build a 144-unit apartment complex for students near Embry-Riddle Aeronautical University in Daytona Beach on nine acres they had previously purchased adjacent to Daytona Memorial Park. But they abandoned that plan and sold the land for $1.7 million. "We decided not to get into construction. That's not what we're best at, and we don't have student housing. We decided to just buy existing apartments," Lowell told the Ormond Beach Observer.

For a few years, they also branded their various apartment complexes with the word, Eagle, in the name, believing it would be advantageous in marketing just as it had been when they had the Lohman name for funeral homes. But the apartment business is not like the funeral home business. Renters aren't necessarily moving to a complex because it's owned by the same company that owns another complex. In fact, it can be a liability. If something happens, and something will happen because of the sheer numbers of apartments and people – a shooting, domestic violence, disputes, tenants unhappy about apartment conditions, police calls, etc. – then having another apartment complex with a similar name isn't necessarily helpful. So, the Lohmans ultimately decided it was best not to continue to use Eagle in the name of every apartment complex they purchased.

Just as had happened when the Lohmans' funeral home and cemetery business grew, apartment investors and large companies started calling, asking if the family was interested in selling. Such was the case in mid-2016. A number of companies wanted to buy four of the apartment complexes the Lohmans owned in the greater Daytona Beach area, and two in Orlando, totaling 1,244 units. When one group of buyers from Miami agreed to pay $63 million, the Lohmans decided it was an offer too good to pass up.

"We didn't intend to sell," Lowell told the Daytona Beach News-Journal. "They weren't on the market."

Before the sale, though, Ty and Lowell had intense discussions about the wisdom of selling versus not selling and continuing to enjoy the thousands of dollars in monthly income these six apartment complexes were generating.

"That was one of the toughest conversations he and I had when I said we needed to sell them," Ty says. "He said, 'We're getting x amount every month and I don't ever want to sell these.' I said, 'Remember, we got all of these out of foreclosure, and this market is coming back really strong. I think we can get this amount for them.' It was like $67 million. 'If you put your money in the market, making ten percent, and now if we have that equity out and invest that, we'll make that much more.' We had a five-day conversation. I said, 'If the market goes backwards, and they're only worth $50 million next year, don't get mad at me.' I wanted to make sure we all understood the risks because we had a lot of money in this thing."

The same newspaper story about the sale also told of the Lohmans' recent purchase of a 148-unit complex in Daytona Beach, and Lowell pointed out that even with the sale of the six complexes, "We are still in acquisition mode."

They now owned eleven apartment complexes with 2,491 apartments.

One person the Lohmans brought into their apartment business was Johanne Brouard, who previously worked in the Lohman's funeral home and cemetery business as an assistant to Ty and Lowell in pre-need sales. For the apartment business, she was selected as chief operating officer, again working directly for Ty and Lowell. She talks with Ty most days and with Lowell once a week or so. She has considerable autonomy, and doesn't believe either of them micromanages. "They do if they need to," she says. The company is successful, she believes, because they are "very smart businessmen," and "they're all about systems and monitoring." They also hired Loucretia Campos, a CPA who serves as their Chief Financial Officer. Together, Lowell says, "They run the company. Loucretia, who has many years of apartment accounting and finance experience, is extremely strong."

One management practice Lowell introduced into the apartment business, as he had done with others in the funeral business, was for Johanne to take one day, usually a Friday, and step back and look at the overall company rather than traveling to individual apartment complexes and getting involved with their day-to-day management and issues. Lowell likens this practice to getting in a helicopter and hovering so you can see all the businesses from a distance, and with a different perspective, and in a different context. He tells her to think of it as "Helicopter Fridays."

"I told her she was down in the trenches too much. She's too important to us for her to be involved in everything that's happening," says Lowell. So, he told her, "I want you to analyze every business we have, and then on Fridays, I don't want you in the trenches. I want you in your helicopter thinking of the entire company, not just one location – and how we can improve."

Lowell also does his own "helicoptering" every day. He and Ty talk about the business nearly daily, but Lowell doesn't want or need to be involved in the nitty-gritty of running the company. Ty does more of that. Lowell delegates and keeps an eye on the big picture. He regularly receives various financial and operational reports, including results from phone shopping. Those are among the most important parts of his system for monitoring the business. He believes those reports provide him a wealth of information about how well the company is doing financially and how well managers and others are performing when it comes to customer service. Also, his philosophy has always been to put the best people in place and let them handle the daily operations.

On occasions, Lowell and Ty go together to visit their properties. They meet with apartment managers, maintenance supervisors and others. Lowell walks the grounds with managers and they discuss what improvements or changes are needed, anything that could be done better, or what's working and what's not working. From all of this comes a written checklist. On a subsequent visit, Lowell always brings his copy of the checklist and reviews it with the manager.

"He wants to see that it was done," says Johanne. Employees know this is important – and if it's not done, they might see a little bit of the "fire-breathing dragon" side of Lowell, although his management style also means ending the conversations by praising them about some other aspect of their work, or at least saying something positive about them, "saving" them or "rescuing" them, as Lowell calls it. Employees, though, usually see the "warmth" side of Lowell's "power and warmth" approach, says Johanne. Still, they know he means business, and sometimes "power" can be interpreted as "fear." "There's fear. They know to respect him, and know what he says to do better get done." Johanne likens it to one of his Lowellisms: "Trust, but verify."

Lowell says, "I think it's important to have a sense of humor. I don't want our staff to be afraid of me, but I want them to know that accountability is there. We have to run a business, but we can run it and have fun, and continue a learning process."

"Every time you're with him, he's teaching you," Johanne says. "I always thought he should have been a teacher. I've learned a lot from him."

The Lohman Apartments training manuals include a Leasing/Marketing Checklist; pages such as Accountability: Get in Your Helicopter!; Phone Shopping Survey questions; and a seven-page maintenance test covering everything from pools to electrical to appliances, air conditioning, plumbing and more. And there is one page featuring a checklist for managers.

"LOWELL'S CHECKLIST"

- Modern Music in offices.
- Clean desks in offices – no nick (sic) knacks.
- No one answering phone?
- Memorize tenant's names.
- Encourage tenants to go to the web and give us a good review, make form and give them form.
- Are we 102% occupied?
- Lights on? Blinds open?
- Are we on Craigslist account? Are we on Postlets listing? Are we on Apartment Guide? Referral letters?
- Leave your desk, greet potential tenants.
- Call them back one hour after they leave.
- Sense of Urgency.
- Come in now.
- Have calls transferred to cell phones.
- If busy, still acknowledge walk ins!
- Don't Want to Do = No Excuses!
- Don't get lazy – Answer Phones, Take Names, Call Back
- Personality/Appearance – Make a good impression. Be positive, get excited!
- When hiring, bring them in now! Do not ask them to send in a resume, and you will call them back later.
- They – your staff – can't by-pass you and go to the owner!
- "Lowellisms"

Lowell says he misses the funeral and cemetery business because he enjoyed it for so many years, but when it comes to ease of operation and making money, the apartment business is superior. And, if one can time the purchases and sales of properties based on the market and going into or out of recessions, the apartment business is one of those nearly recession-proof businesses like the cemetery and funeral business. In the apartment business, there are always people who need to rent, or want to rent, and there are even more of them during recessions or periods of high unemployment when many can't afford to buy a home.

Ty says the apartment business is much more lucrative and also requires less of a hands-on approach than the funeral and cemetery business. "It's a lot easier than the funeral business. It just takes a lot of cash to buy them."

The rewards, though, can also be multiplied.

In late summer 2017, interest in the Lohmans' apartment complexes was heating up. Back in March and April, there were some inquiries from potential buyers considering offering about $113 million. But now, offers were coming in from companies and investors interested in buying the ten Lohman properties in Orlando and Jacksonville. The Lohmans' brokers, Mike Donaldson and Nick Meoli with Marcus and Millichap, received more than six hundred inquiries and more than twenty offers. The highest was $122 million.

With buyers talking that kind of number, it got the attention of Ty and Lowell even though they believed the value of the properties was $130 million to $135 million. Earlier, they hadn't originally planned to sell in the summer of 2017. But as Ty says, "If someone says the right number, everything I have is for sale even though we'd like to keep them." Another recession, he says, might be only a few years away, and "you can't get out during the recession. You've got to get out before, but nobody knows when it is. I hope we're timing it right. I think we are."

When the Lohmans spent $17 million to buy the group of apartment complexes in Daytona Beach – that was when Lowell and Nancy first invested with Ty – they paid $28,000 "per door" in industry parlance, which means per apartment. But since that time, the economy improved, rates stayed low, money was available to be borrowed and competition increased, says Lowell. The result, he says, is "the price per door for the same quality property has now increased to between $50,000 and $70,000."

Rather than sell all ten properties in Orlando and Jacksonville as one group offered for $122 million in August 2017, the Lohmans decided it was best to separate the offerings into two or three groups and they now believe the final sales total will be well above the $130 million rather than $122 million. Almost immediately, they ended up with a $37 million contract from a California company to purchase the three Orlando properties totaling 568 units. That meant a price of more than $65,000 per door. They pushed the closing of the Orlando properties back to January 2018 for tax reasons.

The Lohmans also accepted an offer for three Jacksonville properties totaling $30.6 million for 632 units.

Even though they were actively engaged to sell the Orlando and Jacksonville apartments, they were not getting out of the business. They were looking to buy more in the Daytona Beach area where they still owned one apartment complex. They placed offers to buy two apartment complexes. They presently still own eleven apartment complexes totaling 2,486 apartments in Daytona Beach, Orlando and Jacksonville.

Whether buying or selling, the Lohmans' legal and financial representatives played a huge role in the transactions. Lowell has always believed it's important for business owners to have trusted attorneys and accountants. In all of the Lohmans' transactions, attorney Jeff Brock handled the legal details and accountant Mary Greenlees handled the financial aspects.

Lowell Lohman's Businesses
Solely Owned or Owned with Family

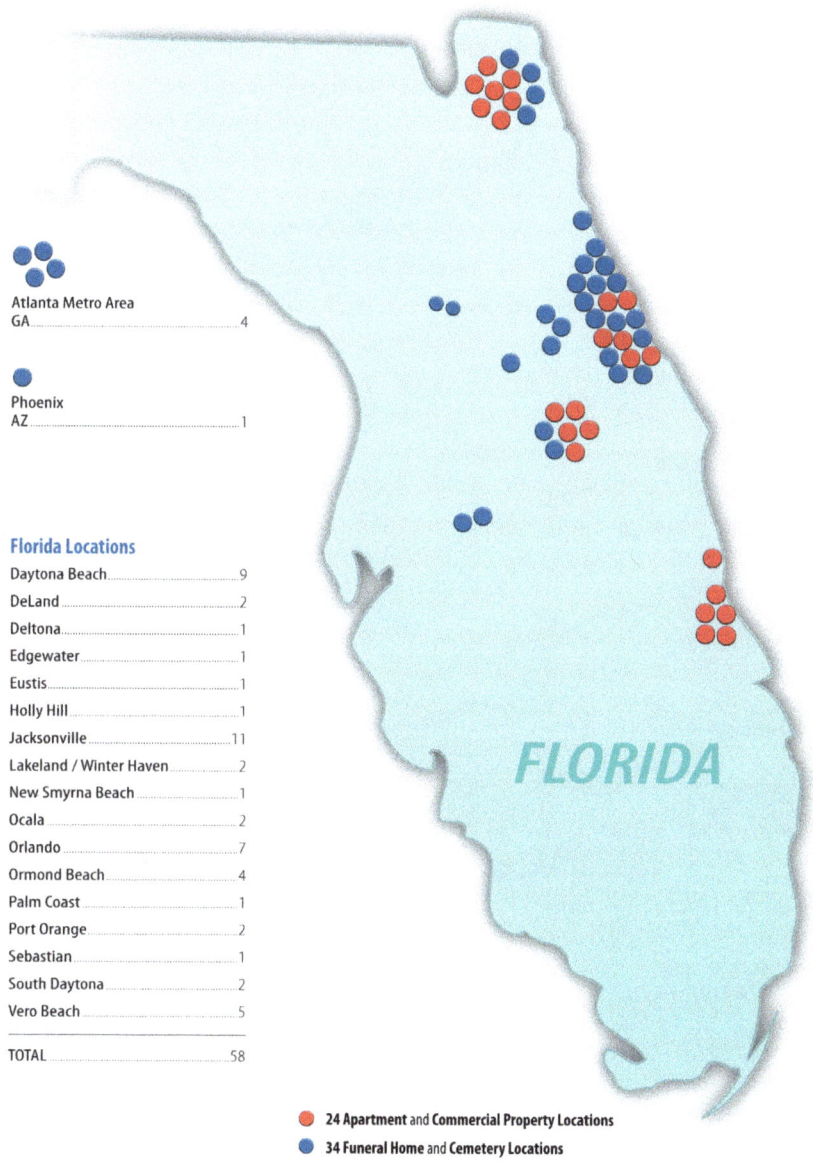

Atlanta Metro Area
GA 4

Phoenix
AZ 1

Florida Locations
Daytona Beach 9
DeLand 2
Deltona 1
Edgewater 1
Eustis 1
Holly Hill 1
Jacksonville 11
Lakeland / Winter Haven 2
New Smyrna Beach 1
Ocala 2
Orlando 7
Ormond Beach 4
Palm Coast 1
Port Orange 2
Sebastian 1
South Daytona 2
Vero Beach 5

TOTAL 58

● 24 Apartment and Commercial Property Locations
● 34 Funeral Home and Cemetery Locations

Funeral and Cemetery Locations

Atlantis Cremation
Daytona Beach, FL

Baggett & Summers Lohman Funeral Home
Daytona Beach, FL

Beaches Memorial Park and Funeral Home [2 locations]
Jacksonville, FL

Cardwell Lohman Funeral Home
Port Orange, FL

Cheatham Hill Memorial Park
Marietta, GA

Cherokee Memorial Park
Cherokee County, GA

Daytona Memorial Park
Daytona Beach, FL

Daytona Memorial Park North
Daytona Beach, FL

DeLand Memorial Gardens
DeLand, FL

Edgewater New Smyrna Cemetery
Edgewater, FL

Eustis Memorial Park
Eustis, FL

Forest Lawn Memorial Park and Funeral Home [2 locations]
Ocala, FL

Glenn Abbey Memorial Park and Funeral Home [2 locations]
Lakeland/Winter Haven, FL

Hillandale Memorial Park
Lithonia, GA

Holly Hill Memorial Park and Funeral Home [2 locations]
Jacksonville, FL

Lohman Funeral Home Daytona
Daytona Beach, FL

Lohman Funeral Home Deland
DeLand, FL

Lohman Funeral Home Deltona
Deltona, FL

Lohman Funeral Home Ormond
Ormond Beach, FL

Lohman Funeral Home Palm Coast
Palm Coast, FL

Lohman Funeral Home Port Orange
Port Orange, FL

Lohman Pet Cemetery & Cremation [2 locations]
Daytona Beach, FL

North Atlanta Memorial Park
Dunwoody, GA

Orlando Memorial Park
Orlando, FL

Royal Vault Company
Orlando, FL

Sun City Memorial Park
Phoenix, AZ

Volusia Crematory
Daytona Beach, FL

Volusia Memorial Park and Funeral Home [2 locations]
Ormond Beach, FL

Apartment & Commercial Property Locations

AIA Utility Company
Vero Beach, FL

Arlington Eagle Apartments
Jacksonville, FL

Camelot Gardens Apartments
Jacksonville, FL

Eagle Bay Apartments
Daytona Beach, FL

Eagle Briar Apartments
New Smyrna Beach, FL

Eagle Court Apartments
Jacksonville, FL

Eagle Landing Apartments
Orlando, FL

Eagle Oaks Apartments
South Daytona, FL

Eagle Park Apartments
Holly Hill, FL

Eagle Point Apartments
Daytona Beach, FL

Eagle Pointe I Apartments
Jacksonville, FL

Eagle Pointe II Apartments
Jacksonville, FL

Eagle Reserve Apartments
Orlando, FL

Eagle Ridge Apartments
Jacksonville, FL

Eagle Summit Apartments
Orlando, FL

Indian River Laboratory
Vero Beach, FL

Indian River Utilities
Vero Beach, FL

Jacksonville Village Apartments
Jacksonville, FL

Lamplighter Mobile Home Park
Sebastian, FL

Lohman Property Management /
Lohman Offices
Ormond Beach, FL

Millennium Eagle Apartments
Orlando, FL

Old Dixie Utility Company
Vero Beach, FL

Orlando Bend Apartments
Orlando, FL

Seminole Shores Subdivision
Vero Beach, FL

Chapter 13

'If You're Giving Back, It's Such a Great Feeling'

"Those who are happiest are those who do the most for others."
Booker T. Washington

After paying off the debt the Lohmans owed on their investments in apartment buildings they have sold, the net was millions and millions of dollars. The question then was what to do with the money, aside from what's used to buy more apartments.

Lowell had an idea.

"Think about how much money we could give away," he told Nancy when they talked about selling the apartments in Jacksonville and Orlando.

"We don't want a jet or a yacht," says Nancy. "We built our dream house here with the sale from the Atlanta and Jacksonville cemeteries. We had this house before we had any Lohman properties, long before we were in business here in Daytona and Ormond Beach.... We have enough."

Their lifestyle and spending still leave room to give away money. And so, they do.

For years, the couple has donated to numerous charitable causes and various organizations. For Lowell, who grew up never thinking about having enough money to give away, the donations began on a small scale in 1989 after he and family members – Irv, Opal, Victor and Daryl – each became millionaires when they sold all of their funeral homes and cemeteries for $13.5 million. Lowell invested most of his share in business, buying cemeteries and ultimately reaping even bigger paydays when he sold them. Then in 2012, when he, Nancy, Victor and Ty sold their company of funeral homes and cemeteries for $25 million, philanthropy came to be an important part of wealth. And, of course, the opportunities to give and the number of requests skyrocketed. But so did the amounts Lowell and Nancy gave. The apartment business is lucrative and that provides them with more money to donate.

To Lowell, being able to give away money is both a joy and an obligation. "This city made us very successful for all those years, particularly in the funeral and cemetery business, and now the apartment business," he says. "If you're giving back, it's such a great feeling." He believes strongly that businessmen and businesswomen, and others who have the financial ability to donate money should do so.

Although some people prefer their donations to be anonymous, the publicly announced acts of charity frequently result in considerable goodwill for a donor's business or company. The Lohmans have experienced that many times. Often, stories about their donations or charitable acts ended up in the newspaper or magazines, or in publications sponsored by governments and organizations. Such was the case when Lowell coordinated with other business owners to purchase Medjool Palm trees to be placed along Ormond Beach's main corridor. Lowell and Nancy had planted four when they built Ormond Funeral Home and that gave Lowell the idea that trees like that could beautify the city. With Lowell's encouragement, other business owners along with the Lohmans purchased a number of the trees for $2,800 each, and Lowell had them planted them at various high-profile intersections. Lowell and Nancy also wondered why Ormond Beach lacked appropriate "Welcome" signs at various entry points to what Nancy calls "our little sparkling city by the sea." Working with city officials who secured appropriate state approval for placement of the signs, Lowell and Nancy donated $50,000, half of the amount needed, to purchase and place six signs: "Welcome to Ormond Beach."

Because of Nancy and Lowell's love for pets – they have two cats, SugarBear and Miss Peanut, and one dog, Snowball – it seemed natural that the Halifax Humane Society in Daytona Beach would become a favorite of the couple, in a big way.

What started in 2016 as Nancy leading a community campaign to raise money for a $3.6 million renovation of the organization's fifty-year-old facility turned into the Lohmans donating $500,000, and then another $300,000 – and they weren't done.

LOWELLISM

Philanthropy
Philanthropy is doing something bigger than yourself. It's about doing something that is meaningful and makes a difference. It is more powerful to give than receive. A lot of people have the ability to give, but don't do it. Shame on them.

In January 2017, stories about their $800,000 in donations and their comments about why they did it appeared in numerous local media outlets. They were quoted, in part, as saying "...our mission is to help our community's animals as well as the many children, families and older adults who live alone. We cherish the role pets play in our lives and the part they play within humanity as an anchor of love; a deep love that touches each of our lives."

Even before they made the large gifts to the Halifax Humane Society, local residents knew of the Lohmans' love for pets because of the pet cemetery and columbarium they established years ago adjacent to Daytona Memorial Park. Plus, the couple had previously been active in fundraising and giving to the humane society. Sometimes the gifts were small, but still greatly appreciated, such as the time they bought a new large-screen television to replace the one that was stolen from the organization's headquarters on Thanksgiving Day.

LOWELLISM

Generosity
Take care of the people that take care of you.

After the $500,000 and $300,000 donations, the organization announced it would rename its main building the Nancy & Lowell Lohman Adoption & Pet Center at Halifax Humane Society. The group's CEO, Miguel Abi-hassan, was quoted in the February 3, 2017 Hometown News as saying the Lohmans "get the big picture" and "they are an inspiration of what an ideal humanitarian should be."

In July 2017, Lowell suggested to Nancy that they give another $200,000. Nancy was thrilled. Their contribution now totals $1 million.

A few of the other organizations to which they have donated money, time, or both:

- Ormond Beach Historical Society: restoration of the

Three Chimneys Sugar Mill Ruins; construction of a sidewalk at the Anderson-Price Memorial Building; and helping to save the MacDonald House.
- Florida Hospital: a granite monument in the healing garden; two swans for the pond near the Comprehensive Cancer Center; and a considerable donation to help create a Well Center.
- Daytona Beach Police Department: a black onyx monument honoring officers killed in the line of duty.
- Father Lopez High School in Daytona Beach: a new football scoreboard.
- Ormond Beach Chamber of Commerce: Nancy served as capital campaign chair; a donation to the office/headquarters renovations; a Medjool Palm tree to the renovated site.
- The Ohio State University: donations to the Alumni Association annually. A bench with a bronze plaque outside the Longaberger Alumni Building reads: Nancy and Lowell Lohman, 1981 Homecoming Queen.
- Bethune-Cookman University: donation of $100,000 to the school's athletic programs and future student center; Nancy was selected to serve on the Board of Trustees beginning in late 2017.
- Council on Aging: annual donations to the COA Living Gifts Foundation.
- Ormond Memorial Art Museum and Gardens: annual donations, including Art in the Garden annual sponsor and annual Heritage Membership level.
- Florida International Festival: sponsor and host for

the bi-annual Daytona Beach area musical program featuring The London Symphony Orchestra.

It's not just organizations that have been recipients. Individuals have benefited, including numerous family members Lowell and Nancy have taken on group vacations to places such as Europe, Canada and New York City.

> *LOWELLISM*
>
> **Kindness**
> Always search for ways to do random acts of kindness.

Many other individuals have benefited directly from the Lohmans' donations whether money was given for a specific cause or randomly to the unsuspecting. Lowell has paid for dental work for probably a half-dozen people, including some employees who couldn't afford the cost for a new look that improved their health and boosted their self-confidence. There are other individuals who are beneficiaries of the Lohman's gifts. And then there are the $100 bills Lowell and Nancy give out frequently. Random acts of kindness, they call it. Sometimes it means an extra bonus for people doing work for the Lohmans, such as window-washing, housekeeping, cleaning the swimming pool at their home, or maintenance or carpentry. Sometimes, it's a server in a restaurant who gets the $100 bill as a tip. Or, it might just be someone who, for whatever reason, really needs extra cash, and it represents a big sum to them. Sometimes the recipient might be someone who's in an unexpected jam.

"It's such a great reaction when you surprise someone with that. There are so many people out there who really need it. One hundred dollars changes a lot of people's lives," Lowell says. Nancy learned this from Lowell (another Lowellism): "A generous tip won't change our lives, but it might change theirs."

"We search for times to do that. It makes you feel great about yourself if it helps them out," says Lowell. "The more you give, the more you get."

Chapter 14

'Jump on These Shoulders and Hang On'

"The chief factor in any man's success
or failure must be his own character."
Theodore Roosevelt

In a career that has spanned more than five decades, and is not over yet, Lowell likes to count the number of businesses he has owned and co-owned. Most have been with family members, including his mother, stepfather, two brothers, son and wife. The total: fifty-eight businesses when counting individual funeral homes, cemeteries, crematoriums, a vault company, a mobile home park, water and sewer treatment facilities, laboratories, a residential subdivision and individual apartment complexes. To Lowell, it's a measure of success when he thinks about the cumulative value of those businesses, which is more than $250 million. Even after subtracting the debt associated with them, Lowell and his family clearly know wealth. They are living the American Dream, at least as it is defined by most people who think of success in terms of business and financial independence. Lowell, of course, looks at it that way, but there is more to it than that. What's important to him, he says, is that the success has revolved around family. Lowell usually has been the one who is the driving force, the dominant, assertive, excitable entrepreneur, always thinking big, always pushing for more, always with a vision of what could be. And always keeping family business top of mind.

> *LOWELLISM*
>
> **Integrity**
> Do the right thing.

From the beginning, he has relied on specific strategies and business practices he values, such as having systems in place, monitoring those systems and evaluating results or the lack of results, monitoring employee performance, having excellent sales ability, picking the right people as partners and managers, and delegating, delegating, delegating. His ownership and management style works, in part, he says, because he is highly structured. He's not detail-oriented, but he says he doesn't want or need to be involved in the details of operating any business. Many of the business principles and practices he puts into place while owning, operating and growing companies are part of most entrepreneurs' playbooks. But just as important, if not more so, are the intangibles Lowell believes are keys to his success, and can be for others. His character and integrity were forged as a child growing up in a loving family. And he developed many of his other traits and values, or at least started developing them, while participating in sports as a boy and as a young man, long before he thought about business.

It's a cliché to talk about how sports can hugely influence boys and girls, and young men and young women, sometimes for the good, sometimes for the bad. Not everyone has good experiences in sports, but in most scenarios, much is learned. And there are numerous books written about what sports can teach: leadership, character, perseverance, discipline, teamwork, sportsmanship, competitiveness, grace in winning, humility in losing. From an early age, Lowell experienced all of them playing baseball, basketball and football. And every lesson learned influenced him throughout his life in his businesses and in his personal relationships. Leadership became the fountain from which many traits and values flowed.

"I think at twelve years old I was teaching," says Lowell. "And through the high school years, your coaches are looking to you to lead those kids because of your athletic ability. If you don't think being the quarterback for your high school football team affects your life, you're wrong. I would think to myself in the huddle, 'I'm getting ready to go to war.' You're playing the other team over there, and your school is in the stands. Over a period of years, you get that attitude – I had that in sports: 'We're going to do this. Just jump on these shoulders and hang on.' I think that's an attitude you have, from a leadership standpoint. I like to think the coaches thought of me as a fourth coach. That molded me pretty quick. I didn't know the business end of it yet, but I knew I had all of those traits in sports. Those were getting molded at an early age, and I just carried them right on into business."

> *LOWELLISM*
>
> **Character**
> Character is what you do when no one is looking.

Other intangible traits that have served him well in business are some of the same he saw in his father, who was not a businessman, but still helped shape Lowell's character for life and business: "outgoing, good personality and a big heart." Empathy, compassion and having respect for others were among the values taught to Lowell and his brothers.

Whether in sports or business, Lowell also believes his competitiveness has played a big part in his business accomplishments. He describes himself, as do others, as a "very competitive creature."

"I like to build businesses. I love the hunt of accomplishing something. I love building something."

Lowell and family members who are, or have been, co-owners of businesses with him can't think of much to say when asked what his weaknesses are as a businessman and entrepreneur. "What am I not good at? I probably don't have as much patience as I've grown older. I think that happens to everybody," he says. Still, his penchant for wanting to get things done now, and always pushing to do more, quicker, and do it better has not usually hampered his relationships. Nor has the occasional "fire-breathing dragon" side of him. "I won't say I have a temper, but it can crawl out."

His brother, Victor, who has a close relationship with Lowell and describes him as his best friend, worked with Lowell in the cemetery and funeral business for more than twenty years. "He got along with people, and treated people well," says Victor. "When it was bad, he'd let them know, but always gave everybody that pat on the back. He also gave them that little kick in the butt if it was needed. He was very good with that, and I'm talking way outside the family to employees. He didn't hesitate jumping into a case if it needed it."

Lowell's brother, Daryl, who was part of the Sloman family-owned funeral and cemetery business, says all of his life he has looked up to Lowell – in business, sports and life. "He's always been an inspiration." For example, Daryl, who was born twelve years after Lowell, says he doubts he would have gone to college and stuck with it if Lowell had not done it.

Daryl observed Lowell's leadership and willingness to take risks, noting that he was "a good delegator and good in structuring things." And both Daryl and Victor equate Lowell's business leadership to being the leader of a football team. "He just always had that quarterback mentality," says Daryl.

Ty, who often responds to his dad by calling him "Sir," describes Lowell as a "tremendous leader" who is good at motivating people. And still today Nancy hears Ty say to his father, "Dad, I need a little bit of wisdom from you." She says it shows how much he respects Lowell.

> *LOWELLISM*
>
> **Be Nice**
> Everybody thinks to be successful in business, you have to be a jerk. That's totally false. You don't have to be.

"He understands people and the psychology of dealing with people. You hear us talking about power and warmth a lot. That is psychology 101 in dealing with people. If you just talk to somebody, it won't sink in with ninety percent of the people. A lot of the power is used, but in the end, you have to come back and save them. Warmth-wise, he says, 'You're better than this. Let's get this done.' Be positive, but get your point across. I think that's the best strength he's got, and his vision.... I am very fortunate to have him as my dad. I got really lucky. I wouldn't be anywhere I am without him. He's the best teacher. I feel like I had Warren Buffet in the house growing up," says Ty.

Of the eight family members who have worked in businesses owned or co-owned by Lowell, only his oldest son, Brian, did not stay in the family business for long. It was never a good fit.

Spouses working together in business can sometimes lead to serious friction not only in the workplace, but at home. Nancy and Lowell say that has never been the case with them. Each recognized the other's unique role in the family businesses, they say. And, of course, Lowell created the funeral and cemetery business based on Nancy being the face of the company and in a position to use her business acumen and sales skills, as well as those intangibles she possesses similar to Lowell's. The best day in his life, he says, was when he met her. And then, to nurture the relationship and marry her, and convince her to be his business partner – those are the smartest decisions he has ever made, he adds. At home, the couple has never felt they have to avoid discussions, or disagreements, about that day's business, or any part of the business. There is no wall between business life and home life.

But surely, there must be areas where they as husband and wife and business partners don't get along or don't see eye-to-eye.

"I'm sure on both sides of the fence, there are things that each other gets annoyed with," says Nancy. "I think with any relationship, you have something you wish the other person would curtail. It's interesting we really don't focus on those; we don't say things like 'you always or never do this' because they're dangerous words in a relationship. I think we both know it's important when to deliver feedback and how."

Nancy and Lowell rave about their marriage. Lowell says of all the people "on the planet," Nancy is the one for him. On Valentine's Day weekend, eight years into their marriage in 1999, the couple was featured in a Daytona Beach News-Journal story entitled, "For happy love, remember to date your mate." They talked about the importance of complimenting each other and making each other feel appreciated. "Showering your spouse with affection makes both of you feel good," Nancy told the newspaper. "It's going to come back tenfold." Lowell was quoted as saying he knows how lucky he is to have found Nancy. "My goal is to be the best husband I can be.... I just love seeing her happy."

> *LOWELLISM*
>
> **Success**
> Success is the freedom to be yourself.

Fittingly, the photo accompanying the story shows Lowell kissing Nancy's cheek as he holds a glass slipper he had given to her because, as the photo caption says, he "likens the story of their meeting to the fairy tale, Cinderella." In 2017, twenty-six years since their wedding day, he still refers to her as Cinderella. And Nancy still loves talking about Lowell.

"These are the things I think makes him an eleven on a scale from one to ten in terms of being a great husband: he boasts and brags about me to others. There's not a woman out there that wouldn't want to hear that all the time. I'm sure our friends get sick of it, but I don't. It's so nice that he does that all the time. He appreciates the little things like saying thank you when I bring him a bottle of water when he's watching TV. He's smart with that because it makes me want to do it even more. He's always so appreciative and complimentary. Then the other thing that he does that's really adorable is he leaves me Post-it Notes, like when I'm going to have a big day, it'll say something like 'so proud of you.' It's so nice, these things.

"We also joke about how someone with a nickname is a fun person.... I think there's a positive correlation between

Lowell with his great personality, likeability and charisma and the fact that he has a zillion nicknames. It's Loachy or Lur – those were his football names. Now, because of the people he teaches and shares his investment strategy with, one of his buddies calls him Captain Vanguard. So, he has these nicknames, and of course, all the girls in the family, we enjoy calling him Lowell Lohman, M-H-M-M-D, for Maximum High Maintenance Master Delegator."

Although Lowell and Nancy have completed their preplanned funeral arrangements, being in the funeral and cemetery business for more than three decades never caused Lowell to be fixated on his own mortality. But he says it did cause him to focus on living and making the most of his life and business. In more than five decades in business, he has made more money than he ever dreamed of, and has been able to give away more than he ever thought possible. The best part of it all, he says, is that it was, and still is, a family business. The way he looks at it is the same way he looks at life: "It is the journey, not the destination that is important."

Sources and References

Barry Farber's Guide to Handling Sales Objections, by Barry Farber, New Jersey: Career Press, 2005.

Cardwell, Baggett and Summers Funeral Home, cardwellfuneral.com.

Cheatham Hill Memorial Park, sourtherncremations.com.

Daryl Lohman, author interview, July, 2017.

Daytona Beach News-Journal, various articles.

Demographics for Ormond Beach and Daytona Beach, Wikipedia.org.

Eagle Portfolio, Orlando, Marcus & Millichap.

Florida Museum, The University of Florida.

Good to Great: Why Some Companies Make the Leap and Others Don't, by Jim Collins, HarperBusiness, 2001.

Hometown News, February 3, 2017.

International Cemetery & Funeral Management magazine, various articles.

ICCFA Magazine

Joanne Brouard, author interview, July, 2017.

Lohman Apartments Eagle Properties, Checklists.

Lohman Funeral Home, Ormond Beach, Florida, author's field notes.

Lohman Funeral Homes, lohmanfuneralhomes.com.

Lowell Lohman, author interviews, March – August, 2017.

Marketline, American Marketing Association, Central Florida Chapter.

Nancy Lohman, author interviews, March – August, 2017.

Napoleon Hill Foundation, naphill.org.

Neighbor John: Intimate Glimpses of JOHN D. ROCKEFELLER in Ormond Beach, by Curt E. Engelbrecht, The Casements Guild in Cooperation with the Ormond Beach Historical Trust, 1993.

New York Times, April 17, 2006, *For a Price, Final Resting Places That Tut Would Find Pleasant,* by Guy Trebay.

Notes and Writings, Lowell Lohman.

Obituary, Edgar Lohman, legacy.com, Cox-Gifford-Seawinds Funeral Home, *TC Palm,* March 12 – 14, 2011.

Obituary, John D. Rockefeller, New York Times, May 24, 1937.

Obituary, Opal "Ope" (Lohman) Silverman, legacy.com, Cox-Gifford-Seawinds Funeral Home, *TC Palm,* February 9 – 11, 2010.

Ormond Beach Historical Society, ormondhistory.org.

Ormond Beach Observer, various articles.

Polio, Centers for Disease Control and Prevention, cdc.gov.

Quarterly meeting, Lohman Apartments Eagle Properties, April 2017, author's field notes.

Random House Webster's Quotationary, by Leonard Roy Frank, Random House, Inc., 2001, 1999.

Random Reminiscences of Men and Events, by John D. Rockefeller, New York: Doubleday Page & Company, 1909.

Recessions, wikipedia.org.

Sales Management Guidelines, Atlanta Division, Lowell Lohman.

Seniors Today newspaper.

Southern Cemetery, Stewart Enterprises, Inc. display ad, May/June, 1993.

Southern Funeral Director.

The Casements, ormondbeach.org.

The Emperor's Handbook: Marcus Aurelius, A New Translation of the Meditations, by C. Scott Hicks and David V. Hicks, Scribner, 2002.

The Petite Shop, petiteshopverobeach.com.

Titan: The Life of John D. Rockefeller, Sr., by Ron Chernow, New York: Random House, Inc., 1988.

Ty Lohman, author interview, June, 2017.

United States Flag & Touch Football Leagues, ustfl.com.

Victor Lohman, author interviews June – July, 2017.

Video, *Lowell Lohman: A Legacy of Power & Warmth*, New Light Media Productions, 2017.

Volusia/Flagler Business Report, June 25, 2010, *Lohman Funeral Homes, Acquisitions savvy decisions boost sales to record high for funeral business*, by Clayton Park.

Volusia/Flagler Business Report, November 29, 2004, *Family-owned funeral and cemetery company melds big-time efficiencies, hometown roots*, by Barry Flynn.

Appendices

Lowell Lohman's Acknowledgements

In addition to his family members, Lowell personally wants to thank the following friends for having such a positive influence on his life!

Rick Baldwin
Bryan Bergens
Sam Block
Jeff Brock
Johanne Brouard
Michelle Carter-Scott
Loucretia Campos
Jim Chisholm
Jack Frost
Roy Gailey
Mary Greenlees
Sheriff Guindi
John Haire
Paul Hamilton
Joe Hampton
Pete Heebner
David Hood
Gale Lemerand
Ken Lucas
Ken Nichols
Ed Peck
Carl Persis
Buddy Provost
Byron (Buddy) Reeves
Edgar Scott
Bill Stephens
Frank Stewart
Gregg Strom
Doug Thomas
Alan Wolfelt

Lowell and Nancy also want to thank Judith Leslie, graphic and website designer, for the properties map; Brenda Trost Photography for the photos on the front cover and the photos of the four Lohmans; and Don Bok Photography for taking several of the photos used in the book.

Important Dates in the Life of Lowell Lohman

February 16, 1945	Born in Vero Beach, Florida.
June, 1963	Graduated from Vero Beach High School.
May, 1969	Graduated from Florida State University.
1973	Became an entrepreneur with the purchase of his first business: Davis Industries Franchise/Distributor.
1977-1989	Bought and/or built 9 cemetery and funeral home locations along with his brothers, Victor Lohman and Daryl Lohman, his stepfather, Irv Silverman, and his mother, Opal Silverman.
1982	Won the National Flag Football Championship and was inducted into the U.S. Touch and Flag Football Hall of Fame.
1989	Sold 9 cemetery and funeral home locations for $13.5 million.
October 10, 1991	Married Nancy Schaible (Shively).
1989-1996	Bought, built and sold 7 cemeteries and funeral homes in Florida, Georgia and Arizona. They were all owned solely by Lowell Lohman.
August 30, 1998	Lohman Funeral Home Ormond opened.
1998-2012	Bought and/or built 14 cemetery and funeral home locations along with his wife, Nancy; son, Ty; and brother, Victor Lohman.
1977-2012	Throughout this time period, owned and operated 34 cemeteries and funeral homes, the largest private owner of cemeteries and funeral homes in Florida.

July 31, 2012	Sold 14 cemetery and funeral home locations for $25 million.
2013-2016	Purchased 17 apartment complexes totaling 3,700 apartment units with his son Ty Lohman and his wife Nancy.
August, 2016	Sold 6 apartment complexes for $63 million.
Currently	Owns 11 apartment complexes totaling 2,486 apartment units.
Summary	Lowell has owned and operated, some individually and some with family members, a total of 58 operations/locations.

Summary of Achievements of Lowell Lohman

Sports

High School

- Baseball record: .509 batting average
- Captain and quarterback of the football team
- Voted "Most Athletic" by classmates
- Head baseball coach along with Paul Hamilton of Vero Beach's state champion Pony League team. They also coached Vero Beach's state champion American Legion team

College

- Voted Captain and most valuable baseball player by his teammates
- Set school record by striking out 19 batters in one game

Flag Football

- State Champions 3 times
- Voted most valuable player in the state tournament 3 times
- Inducted into the Florida Flag Football Hall of Fame twice
- Won the National Championship
- Voted most valuable player in the national championship twice
- Inducted into the U.S. Touch and Flag Football Hall of Fame
- Played or coached on six state or national championship teams in two different sports

Business

- Largest private owner of funeral homes and cemeteries in Florida
- Owned 34 funeral homes and cemeteries in Florida, Georgia and Arizona
- Awarded a lifetime Achievement Award by the Florida Cemetery, Cremation and Funeral Association
- Owned 17 apartment complexes totaling 3,700 units
- Has owned a total of 58 businesses
- 2000, Lowell and Nancy receive the "Lowell and Nancy Lohman Day" proclamation award from the city of Ormond Beach for the Medjool Palm beautification project Lowell spear-headed
- 2006, Nancy receives the Volusia/Flagler Business Report Five Most Influential Women in Business Award along with four other businesswomen
- 2010, Lowell, Nancy, Victor and Ty Lohman receive the Volusia County Sheriff's Department "Honorary Deputy Sheriff for the Day" Award for their contributions to memorialize and honor the fall officers of Volusia County
- 2005, Lowell, Nancy, Victor and Ty Lohman receive the City of Daytona Beach Beautification Award for transforming Daytona Memorial Park through multiple improvement projects
- 2013, Lowell and Nancy receive the Florida Police Chiefs Association Award for their annual Police Memorial Service at Daytona Memorial Park
- 2015, Lowell and Nancy receive the Ormond Beach Mayor's Award for Civic Engagement for all they have contributed to Ormond Beach, in particular, their passion and their financial donation for welcome signage at the entrances of Ormond Beach
- 2015, Nancy receives the Embassy of Hope Hall of Fame Award for Community Service

Index

A
Aiken, Bob, 28
Asher, Bud, 111
Ashton, Carl, 41-43, 45-46
Aurelius, Marcus, 115

B
Baldwin, Rick, 89, 207
Barrett, Ken, 99
Bergens, Bridget, 158
Bergens, Bryan, 207
Block, Sam, 207
Braun, John, 96
Brock, Jeff, 152, 180, 207
Brouard, Johanne, 175-177, 207

C
Campos, Lucretia, 175, 207
Carter-Scott, Michelle, 207
Chisholm, Jim, 207
Churchill, Winston, 163
Collins, Jim, 17
Collyer, Bryan, 161
Crow, Gene, 48

D
Davis, Forbes, 36-37
Donaldson, Mike, 179
Drucker, Peter, 11, 79

E
Epictetus, 33

F
Frey, Mary, 72-73
Frost, Jack, 207

G
Gailey, Roy, 158, 161, 207

Gailey, Sherry, 158
Greenlees, Mary, 180, 207
Guerin, Stevie, 100
Guindi, Sheriff, 207

H
Haire, John, 207
Hamilton, Paul, 207
Hampton, Joe, 207
Heebner, Nan, 158
Heebner, Pete, 207
Heffner, Ernie, 136
Hill, Napoleon, 93
Holland, Jesse, 24, 98
Holland, Opal Mae, (mother), 23
Holland, Sarah, 24
Hood, David, 111, 207
Hood, Lory, 158
Huggins, Tina, 29, 33
Hughes, Valerie, 87
Hunsaker, Christine, 74

J
Jefferson, Thomas, 21
Johnson, Ashley, 107

K
Kiam, Victor, 49
Koenigs, Chase, 107
Koenigs, Leanne, 107
Koenigs, Matt, 107
Krause, Mark, 136

L
Lemerand, L. Gale, 16, 207
Lohman, Bobby, 25
Lohman, Brian, 33, 38, 61-62, 197
Lohman, Christopher, 83, 103, 161
Lohman, Daryl, 23, 38, 58-61, 65-66, 101, 144, 161, 186, 196-197
Lohman, Edgar, (father), 23-24, 29, 34, 37-38, 104
Lohman, Edmund, 25
Lohman, Lowell
    Birth, 23

    Businesses Owned, Summary, 181-183
    Childhood, 21-28, 98
    College, 28-31, 33-38
    Divorce, 62
    Important Dates in Life of, 209-210
    Lowellism, 46, 51-52, 187-188, 190, 194-197, 199
    Lowell's Insight, 13-15, 18, 26, 29, 34-35, 40, 44-45, 47, 56, 58, 65, 79-81, 86-87, 113, 131, 166, 172
    Marriage, 33, 87, 156
    Philanthropy, 127, 185-191
    Sales Tips, 51-55, 63-64, 82-85, 177-178
    Sports, 21-24, 27-31, 33-34, 37, 61-62, 99-103, 194-195
    Summary of Achievements, 211-212
Lohman, Nancy, 12, 14, 19, 87, 89-91, 93-97, 107, 110, 114, 116-117, 119-120-126, 128, 130-134, 136, 138-142, 148, 150-153, 155-156, 158-162, 164-165, 167-169, 172-173, 179, 185-190, 197-200
Lohman, Opal, (mother), 23-24, 27, 29, 34, 37-38
Lohman, Tina, 33, 38, 41-42, 44-45, 62
Lohman, Tovah, 12
Lohman, Ty, 12, 14, 19, 41, 61-62, 75, 83, 103, 115-116, 120, 122, 131-132, 136, 140-142, 148, 150-155, 158, 161, 165-167, 169-172, 174-176, 179
Lohman, Victor, 21-23, 37-38, 47-50, 55-58, 61, 65-66, 75, 83, 98, 101, 103, 115-116, 119-120, 122-124, 131-132, 136, 141-142, 144, 148, 150, 152, 158, 165, 167, 169, 186, 196
Lucas, Ken, 207
Lucas, Laurentia, 158

M
Manning, Doug, 136
McAree, Mary, 158
McCann, Greg, 142
Meoli, Nick, 179

N
Nancy's Insight, 139, 164
Nichols, Ken, 161, 207
Nicklaus, Jack, 13
Nietzsche, Friedrich, 121

O
Odom, Jim, 45

P
Peck, Hilda, 125
Peck, Sr., Edwin, 125-126, 207
Persis, Carl, 161, 207
Persis, Susan, 158
Provost, Buddy, 207

R
Reeves, Byron (Buddy), 207
Ries, Andrew, 107
Rockefeller, John D., 39, 109-111
Roosevelt, Theodore, 193

S
Schaffter, Marilyn, 107
Schaffter, Richard, 107
Scott, Edgar, 161, 207
Shively, Nancy (Schaible), 71-77, 79-80, 86-87, 157
Silverman, Irv, 37-38, 45, 47-48, 56, 59-60, 66, 94, 104, 144, 186
Silverman, Opal Lohman, 37-38, 47, 60, 66, 104, 144, 186
Simpkins, Jill, 158
Sinatra, Frank, 70
Smith, Carolyn, 107
Smith, Darrin, 107
Smith, Hallie, 107
Stansbury, Glenda, 136
Stephens, Bill, 158, 161, 207
Stephens, Jill, 158
Stephens, Jim, 118
Stewart, Frank, 207
Stobierski, Stan, 87
Strom, Gregg, 168, 207
Summers, Larry, 127

T
Taylor, Elizabeth, 23
Thomas, Doug, 207

W
Washington, Booker T., 185
Weiss, Ann, 107
Wolfelt, Alan, 207

About the Author

E.L. Wilks is a biographer, editor and president of Legacies & Memories, a biography firm that writes, produces and publishes books for individuals, families and businesses. He has written, co-written and edited numerous books.

Books by Legacies & Memories Include:

- *To Win in Business...Bet on the 'Jockey'*
- *Sand in Their Calculators and Other Business Insights*
- *The Harder You Work, The Luckier You Become*
- *The First 80 Years: The Cary M. Maguire Story*
- *Adventures in Life and Business: The Story of James D. Griffin, Sr.*
- *One Speed Wide Open: A Memory of the Life and Times of R. Keith Elliott*
- *Mary Jo… "Tells It Like It Is"*
- *A Legacy of Trust: The Story of FCCI*
- *Chief Servant: The Life and Leadership of Dr. Oswald P. Bronson, Sr.*
- *Living a Life of Gratitude*
- *'Play Good Ball' – and Other Life Lessons: The G.W. Jacobs Story*
- *The Life and Times of J. Robert Peterson*
- *Living Life Large: The Story of Jim Yonge*
- *Achieve Success the Old-Fashioned Way: Earn It*
- *Potatoes, Cabbage, and the Coast: A Florida Farm Family Memoir*
- *The Life of Bob Scherr*

Contact
www.LegaciesandMemories.com
info@LegaciesandMemories.com
(888) 862-2754

Producing Books Since 1999

**Books Published
by Legacies & Memories Include:**

Big-Hearted Charlie Runs The Mile by Krista Keating-Joseph
Anastasia Island: St. Augustine's Jewel by the Sea
by Kenneth M. Barrett, Jr.
The Olde South: A Photo Journey Along the Back Roads of the South
by Rick McAllister
St. Augustine: Unique Places...Disappearing Spaces
by Nancy Macri
Color Me History! St. Augustine, Florida: The Oldest City in the United States by Randy Cribbs
One in a Million: A True Story by Miriam by Miriam Hodges and Holly Rubin Sills
Four Paws Rumble and Tumble Through the Streets in St. Augustine
by Linda R. Beall
Well of Bones: 20 American Snipers, 10,000 ISIS Terrorists
by Peter Guinta
Coffee with Linda: 365 Days of Devotions by Linda M. Brandt
A Squirrel Afraid of Heights? Are You Kidding Me?
by Robert H. Maynard
Jed Chance: Ride For Justice by Arthur Mendenhall

Contact
www.LegaciesandMemoriesPublishing.com

www.ingramcontent.com/pod-product-compliance
Lightning Source LLC
Chambersburg PA
CBHW040328300426
44113CB00020B/2684